THE ROUGH GUIDE TO
Violin
& Viola

**Whether you're a beginner or a pro,
whether you are about to buy a violin
or you want to learn more about the one
you already have − this book is for you.**

Hugo Pinksterboer

THE ESSENTIAL TIPBOOK

Publishing Details

This first edition published September 2000 by Rough Guides Ltd,
62–70 Shorts Gardens, London WC2H 9AB

Distributed by the Penguin Group:
Penguin Books Ltd, 27 Wrights Lane, London W8 5TZ
Penguin Putnam, Inc., 375 Hudson Street, New York, NY 10014
Penguin Books Australia Ltd, 487 Maroondah Highway, PO Box
257, Ringwood, Victoria 3134, Australia
Penguin Books Canada Ltd, 10 Alcorn Avenue, Toronto, Ontario,
Canada M4V 1E4
Penguin Books (NZ) Ltd, 182–190 Wairau Road, Auckland 10,
New Zealand

Typeset in Glasgow and Minion to an original design by
The Tipbook Company bv

Printed in The Netherlands by Hentenaar Boek bv, Nieuwegein

135pp

A catalogue record for this book is available from the British
Library.
1-85828-651-4

THE ROUGH GUIDE TO
Violin
& Viola

Written by

Hugo Pinksterboer

THE ESSENTIAL TIPBOOK

787.2/407413

Rough Guide Tipbook Credits

Journalist, writer and musician **Hugo Pinksterboer** has written hundreds of articles and reviews for international music magazines. He is the author of the reference work for cymbals (*The Cymbal Book*, Hal Leonard, US) and has written and developed a wide variety of musical manuals and courses.

Illustrator, designer and musician **Gijs Bierenbroodspot** has worked as an art director in magazines and advertising. While searching in vain for information about saxophone mouthpieces he came up with the idea for this series of books on music and musical instruments. Since then, he has created the layout and the illustrations for all of the books.

Acknowledgements

Concept, design and illustrations: Gijs Bierenbroodspot

Translation: MdJ Copy & Translation

Editor: Kim Burton

IN BRIEF

Have you just started to play the violin or viola? Are you thinking about buying one? Or do you already have one and want to know more about it? If so, this book will tell you all you need to know about buying or renting a violin, about tailpieces, bridges and fingerboards, and bows, strings and tuning. It also covers the best way to look after your instrument, the history of the violin and the members of the violin family. And a lot more.

Getting the most from your violin

That knowledge will help you make a good choice when you go to buy a violin or viola. If you already have one, then read this Rough Guide to get the most out of it. This book also explains all the jargon you're likely to come across, making it much easier for you to read more about the violin and viola, in books, magazines and brochures, or on the Internet.

Begin at the beginning

If you have only just started playing, or haven't yet begun, pay special attention to the first four chapters. Those who have been playing for longer can skip ahead to chapter 5 if they prefer. Unless it's otherwise stated, references to 'violins' are also applicable to violas.

Glossary

Most of the violin terms you'll come across in this book are briefly explained in the glossary at the end. It also doubles as an index.

CONTENTS

1. THE VIOLIN AND VIOLA

Practising the violin is something you usually do alone. Performing, on the other hand, you'll usually do with others, whether in an orchestra, with twenty or thirty other violinists, or in a string quartet with two violins, a viola and a cello. Or in a band, perhaps one playing jazz or folk. This chapter is about the range of things a violin can do, about violinists, and about what makes it so much fun.

The violin produces a sound when you draw a bow across the strings. That's why it's called a *bowed instrument*, although it's usually known as a *string instrument*. The viola has the same construction, but because it's bigger it sounds lower in pitch.

All kinds of styles

Most violinists play classical music, but you'll find them playing other styles too: the folk music of many different countries, gypsy music and Jewish klezmer, tango and Turkish music, but also the blues, Cajun and country. Stephane Grapelli was a world-famous jazz violinist, Jean-Luc Ponty achieved fame with his jazz-rock records, and Vanessa Mae has even made the charts with her electric violin.

Classical

Classical violin music is widely varied. After all, the instrument has been around for four hundred years, and practically every composer of note since then has written music for it.

violin

viola

A viola is slightly bigger than a violin

Large orchestra

If you play classical music, you'll often do so in a symphony orchestra, a chamber orchestra or even a string orchestra. Such orchestras contain other string instruments, for instance cellos. A cello looks like rather like a large violin, and because of its size, cellists hold the instrument vertically, supporting it on the floor and gripping it between their knees. The double bass, which sounds even lower than the cello, is the biggest string instrument of all. Besides the *strings* (a common name for violins, violas, cellos and double basses) you'll find many other instruments in this kind of orchestra, ranging from clarinets and trumpets to horns, flutes, drums and timpani.

Thirty violinists

Because violins aren't very loud but are vital to the sound of a symphony orchestra, there are more of them than any other instrument. A typical orchestra might have sixteen violinists, and some have more than thirty.

First and second violins

Those violinists are always divided into two groups: the first and second violins. Although each is equally important to the sound of the orchestra, the first violins are often given the melody while the seconds play more of a supporting role. It isn't always the case though.

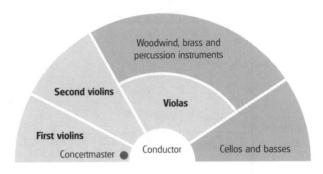

This is how large orchestras are often arranged, with the string instruments at the front.

The violists

The viola players, also known as *violists*, have their own role. The different string *sections* are not unlike the different groups of singers in a choir. A large orchestra may have sixteen viola players.

Leaders

The strings are always at the front, around the conductor. To the conductor's left, right at the front, is the *leader* or *concertmaster* who is responsible for keeping the whole orchestra under control. The second violins and the violas each have their own leaders as well. The louder instruments, such as the trumpets and percussion, sit towards the back.

String quartet

As well as many works for large orchestras, a lot of classical music involving string instruments has been written for smaller groups. String quartets, for instance, which consist of two violinists, a viola player and a cellist, or piano trios, written for violin, cello and piano.

Duo and solo

There is also a lot of music for duos, often a violinist and a pianist. And there are even pieces for unaccompanied solo violin. There is also plenty of music written for a solo violin accompanied by an orchestra.

A few bars from a string quartet (W. A. Mozart); music for two violins, viola and cello

Violin or viola?

Many viola players started out by playing the violin. Only later did they discover that they preferred the sound of a viola. Others began on viola straightaway. If you make the switch later, the viola will take a bit of getting used to, although the principle of playing it is much the same.

2. A QUICK TOUR

A violin has a body, a neck and a fingerboard, four strings, four pegs and many other components. This chapter tells you what everything's called, how to identify it and what it's for, as well as describing the differences between violins and violas, and introduces specially sized violins for children.

The violin pictured on the next page looks much like a violin made a hundred or more years ago. A viola is bigger, and is tuned lower in pitch – that's the only major difference between the two instruments. You can also get violins and violas made in small sizes to suit children, with their small hands and reach. You can read more about them on page 13.

Body
The main part of the violin, the body, is also called the *soundbox*. The *belly* and the *back* of the body are noticeably arched. The belly has two *f*-shaped *sound-holes* or *f-holes*.

Pegs
You tune the strings using the *pegs* or *tuning pegs*, one for each string. These four wooden pegs fit into the *pegbox* at the top of the instrument.

Scroll
At the very top is the *scroll*. In place of a scroll or *volute*, you sometimes see the head of a lion, a woman or an angel, especially on old violins.

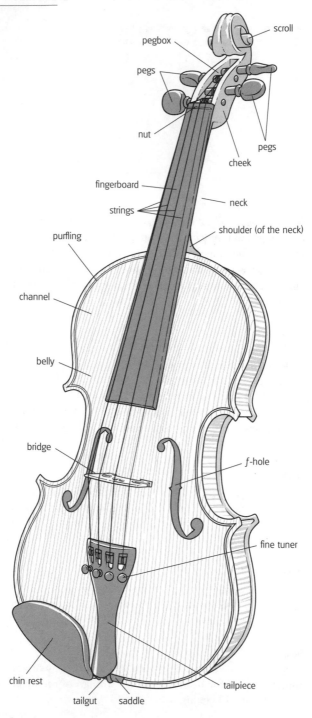

scroll

pegbox

pegs

nut

pegs

cheek

fingerboard

strings

neck

purfling

shoulder (of the neck)

channel

belly

bridge

f-hole

fine tuner

chin rest

tailgut

saddle

tailpiece

Neck and fingerboard

The *neck* lies between the body and the scroll, and glued to the neck is the *fingerboard*, a thin plank of hard dark wood. The fingerboard is quite a bit longer than the neck: a large part juts out over the body. You make the strings produce the note you want by pressing them down, or *stopping* them, at different points along the fingerboard.

Nut

At the top of the fingerboard, the strings run over a small ridge called the *nut.*

The bridge

About halfway down the body the strings run over the *bridge*, a small, elaborately carved piece of wood much lighter in colour than the rest of the violin. When you play, you're actually making the strings vibrate with your bow. The bridge passes on those vibrations to the belly, which, together with the rest of the body, makes sure the instrument will be heard: it amplifies the sound.

Rounded top

The top of the bridge is rounded so that it has almost exactly the same shape as the top of the fingerboard. If the bridge and fingerboard were flat (as they are on a classical guitar), you wouldn't be able to bow the two inside strings without touching the others.

Feet

The bridge stands on the belly on its two *feet*, without the help of glue or screws. The pressure of the strings is enough to make sure it doesn't fall over.

Tailpiece and fine tuners

The strings are attached to the pegbox at one end and to the *tailpiece* at the other. The strings are often hooked onto one or more *fine tuners* screwed into the tailpiece: these are simple devices with small, serrated knobs (*thumb-screws*) which allow you to fine-tune your violin more easily than with the big wooden tuning pegs.

Tailgut, end-button and saddle

The tailpiece is attached to the *end-button* with a loop

known as the *tailgut*. To make sure this tailgut doesn't damage the body, it runs over the *saddle* or *bottom nut*.

Under your chin...

Near the tailpiece you'll also find the *chin rest*. Because there are as many different chins as there are people, chin rests come in all shapes and sizes.

... and on your shoulder

On the other side, against the back of the violin, is a *shoulder rest* or sometimes simply a pad. This makes the violin sit a little higher up your shoulder and more comfortable to play. Even so, violinists still need to tilt their heads to the left a little to hold the violin steady.

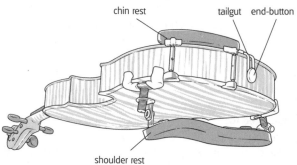

chin rest   tailgut   end-button

shoulder rest

Purfling

The *purfling* runs along the edge of the body. It is usually made of three strips of wood (dark, light and dark).

Channel

From the edge, the belly usually dips a little, before the upward *arching* begins. This 'valley' is called the *channel*. The back is almost the same shape.

Heel and shoulder

The semicircular protrusion at the top of the back is called the *heel*. The *shoulder*, the wider bottom part of the neck, is glued to the heel.

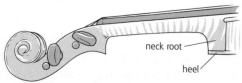

neck root

heel

Violin or viola?

If you compare a violin to a viola, the obvious difference is that the viola is a little bigger. But there are other differences. A violin seems a little slimmer than a viola, and violas are often deeper too: the sides, or *ribs*, are higher. Another difference is that violas sometimes have a kind of 'step' near the pegbox.

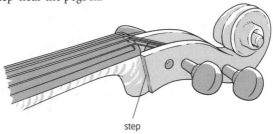

step

A 'step' by the pegbox sometimes serves to distinguish a viola from a violin

INSIDE

There are a number of objects inside the violin as well: the soundpost, bass-bar, blocks and the maker's label.

The soundpost

If you peer through the *f*-hole by the thinnest string, you will see a length of round wood just under the bridge, wedged between the belly and the back. That's the *soundpost*. Without it, a violin would sound very thin or hollow.

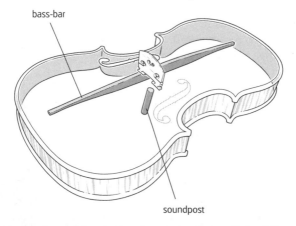

bass-bar

soundpost

The bass-bar and soundpost are important to the sound of a violin.

The bass-bar

Near the other *f*-hole, on the opposite side of the bridge, is the *bass-bar*, which strengthens the belly, and brings out the lowest vibrations of a violin (the bass tones).

The label

You'll only be able to see a tiny part of the bass-bar, by looking from the side and peering through the top part of the *f*-hole. If you look straight down through the same hole, you may well see the maker's label.

Blocks

A violin has thin strips of wood glued along its inside edges, plus wooden blocks in the corners in the middle of the body, by the neck and by the *tail* (the bottom), which serve to make the instrument more sturdy.

THE BOW

To play your violin you need a bow, which is almost as important as the instrument itself.

Ribbon and stick

A bow has a *ribbon* made up of around a hundred and fifty hairs. Those hairs almost always come from a horse's tail. One end of the ribbon is held in place inside the *tip* or *head*, at the top end of the *stick* or *bow stick*. The other end of the ribbon is fixed inside the *frog*.

Tension

Before you play, you have to tighten (*tension*) the ribbon. To do so, you turn the *adjuster, end screw* or *screw button* to move the frog backwards until there's

head

stick

ribbon

winding

lapping

frog

adjuster

about 0.25" (5–6mm) between the ribbon and the middle of the stick. After you have finished playing, turn the adjuster in the other direction until the ribbon goes slack.

Lapping

At the place where you hold the bow you will see the protective *lapping*, *thumb grip* or *bow grip*, often made of leather, and a *winding*, usually of very thin metal wire. These give you a better grip on the stick and help protect the wood.

Rosin

For the bow to do its job properly, you need to rub the ribbon with a piece of *violin rosin*. This makes it slightly sticky when you play. If you don't, the bow will slide across the strings without producing a sound.

STRINGS AND CLEFS

Both violin and viola have four strings. These strings may be made of steel, gut or synthetic material. The thicker ones are usually wound with ultra thin metal wire.

G, D, A, E

The lowest sounding string of a violin is tuned to the note G below middle C. Next to it is the D-string, followed by the A, and the thinnest, highest-sounding string is the E. If you are familiar with the piano keyboard, you will notice that the difference between the note one string is tuned to and the next is represented by five white keys (from G to D, for example). That difference in pitch, or *interval*, is called a *fifth*. A *perfect fifth*, to be exact.

Fifths

You can hear that interval if you sing *Twinkle, Twinkle, Little Star*: the second *Twinkle* is a perfect fifth higher than the first.

C, G, D, A

The highest three strings on a viola are tuned to the same notes as the lowest three on a violin: G, D, and A. You can see that clearly on the piano keyboard shown on page 12. The lowest sounding string of the viola is tuned to C.

Violin music on paper

Violin music is written on a five-line *staff* marked with the G clef, also called the *treble clef*. The tail of this curly symbol (a stylized letter G) circles the second line from the bottom, indicating that the note written on it is a G. This G sounds an octave higher than the lowest note you can play on a violin. That low G is written below this staff using *leger lines*.

The viola clef

The lowest note of a viola (the C) comes quite a way below this staff. You would need four leger lines to write it, which would make these low notes hard to read. That's why viola music is written in a different clef: the *C clef*. Both clefs are used in the music example on page 4.

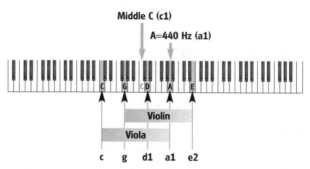

Tuning to "A"

The A-string of a violin is tuned to the note A found just to the right of the middle of a piano keyboard. In musical

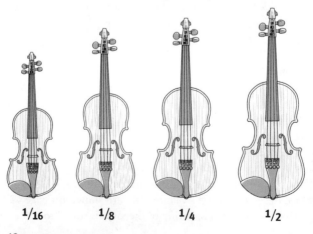

1/16   1/8   1/4   1/2

convention this is called *a1*. This is also the note that most musicians use as a reference when tuning their instruments.

SMALL VIOLINS

A normal violin is too big for most children under twelve, so makers produce violins in small or *fractional sizes* for them. Violas also come in children's sizes.

Full-size violin

An 'adult' violin is called a *full-size violin*. On paper, this is often shown as 4/4. One of the smallest fractional sizes, the 1/16, is actually about half the size of a full-size instrument. Violins can come in 1/10 and other 'in-between' sizes as well as the sizes shown here.

A half or a quarter

There is no absolute rule to help match the size with the age of the player. One six-year-old might be better off with a quarter-size violin, another with a half-size, so it's very important to try out the instrument, and bow as well, for suitability. A teacher will know how to do this, and so will a good salesperson or someone who rents violins. It's not simply height and length that need to be taken into account, but things like how strong your fingers are as well.

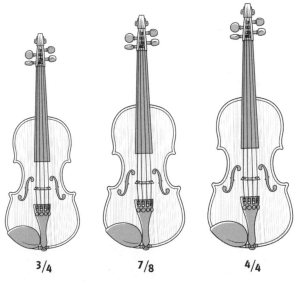

3/4   7/8   4/4

String length

Small violins may differ from one another in string length. The string length, also called the *stop length*, *scale* or *speaking length*, is actually the part of the string between the nut and the bridge. A half-sized violin with a sizeable string length might be the best choice for 'half-sized' violinists with fairly big hands.

3. LEARNING TO PLAY

Is playing the violin difficult, or not? Well, the violin is not the easiest of instruments to start on, but it won't take years of work before you can perform on it. This chapter is about learning how to play, lessons and practising.

To start with, you need to get used to holding the instrument between your chin and your shoulder, and you'll initially feel your left hand is bent at an odd angle when you press the strings down.

Bowing

When you start out, bowing the strings isn't easy either. Wobbly notes are very normal – in fact, you may not even make any sound at all to begin with. In other words, you'll need to master the bowing technique. As well as bowing, you can play the violin by plucking the strings with your fingers. This technique is known as *pizzicato*, and many teachers start their pupils off with pizzicato to get them accustomed to using the left hand before moving on to the bow.

By ear

When you start, you have to learn to press down or *stop* the strings at exactly the right place along the fingerboard. That's far from easy because there are no markers on the fingerboard to tell you where you are. You have to do it 'by feel' and by ear – and that takes practice.

In tune

If you don't press down a string in exactly the right place, it will sound out of tune. Learning to play in tune on a violin takes a while, but with a little talent you'll make plenty of progress within a year.

Finding the exact place...

LESSONS

Hardly anyone learns to play violin without lessons. A teacher won't just show you how to play; a lot of lesson time is also devoted to subjects such as reading music, good bowing technique, attaining a good sound, and good posture.

Trial lesson

If you want to take lessons, ask if you can have a trial lesson first. Then you can see if it clicks between you and the teacher. And between you and the violin!

Not classical

Most violinists concentrate on classical music, and most violin teachers only give 'classical' violin lessons. So if you'd prefer to play another style besides or instead of classical, look for a teacher who is able to (and wants to) teach you.

Locating a teacher

Violin makers and rental firms can refer you to a teacher, and music shops may have a teacher on their staff. You can also ask your local Musicians' Union, or a music teacher at a high school or music college in your area. Also check the classified ads in newspapers, music magazines, on super-market bulletin boards and in shop windows, and try the *Yellow Pages*.

Group or individual tuition?

While most violin students take individual lessons, you could also opt for group tuition if it's available in your area.

Personal tuition is more expensive, but it can be tailored to your exact needs. Professional teachers usually charge around £15–30/$20–50 per hour for individual lessons.

Collectives and music schools
You may also want to check whether there are any teacher's collectives or music schools in your vicinity. These may offer you the chance of ensemble playing, masterclasses and clinics as well as normal lessons, and can be considerably cheaper.

Listening and playing
And finally: listen to the music you would like to play as much as you can, and listen to other music too, on CDs or on the radio, but best of all at concerts. One of the crucial ways to learn to play is to watch other musicians at work. Whether they are living legends or local amateurs, you can learn something from every performance. But the best way of all is to play as often as you can, and practice hard.

PRACTICE
You can play without learning to read music. You can learn without a teacher. But there's no substitute for practice.

How long?
How long you need to practice depends on how gifted you are and what you want to achieve. Playing for thirty minutes to an hour each day will help you make good progress.

Playing a little quieter
Violins aren't terribly loud instruments, but they can make enough noise to bother other people when you are practising. There are ways to avoid this. First of all, you can buy a *practice mute* for your violin, available from as little as £3/$5. This device, which fits onto the bridge of your violin, effectively mutes most of the sound you produce. You can read all about mutes in chapter 8.

Tissue paper
If you lay a paper tissue over the body, the sound will become softer still. What's more, the rosin which comes off the bow as you play won't land on your violin, which lessens

the need for cleaning. You can use the practice mute to fix the tissue to the bridge.

Silent violin

If you need to play more softly still, and money is no object, you can get a *silent violin*. This is a violin without a sound-box, so you can even practice in the middle of the night without disturbing anyone. Prices start at around £250/$350. One drawback is that you can hardly hear a thing yourself. The solution to this problem is an electric violin with a *jack* or socket for a pair of headphones, so you can hear everything while everyone else hears nothing. You can read more about electric violins on pages 103 and 104.

A silent violin

On CD

Playing violin music usually involves more than one musician: other strings, piano or a full orchestra. There's an easy way to get hold of those other musicians: buy a CD or CD-ROM. For instance, you can buy special practice CDs with the same piece of music recorded three times. The first time it is performed very slowly by piano and violin, so that you can play along with the violin part to guide you. The next time it's a bit faster with just the piano part recorded, and the final version is with full orchestra and at the proper tempo. Sheet music is usually included with these CDs.

Lessons on your computer

If you have a computer handy, there are CD-ROMs you can play along to. Some of these will let you set the speed of the piece and choose whether the violin part is heard or not.

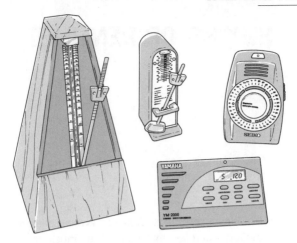

Two mechanical (clockwork) and two electronic metronomes

Metronome

Most pieces of music are supposed to be played in the same tempo from beginning to end. Practising with a metronome now and again will help you to play at a constant speed. A metronome, whether clockwork or electronic, produces ticks or bleeps in the tempo you select, helping you notice if you inadvertently speed up or slow down.

Recording

If you record your violin lessons, you can listen to the whole lesson again when you get home to review what was said, and especially how you – or the teacher – sounded. It's actually much easier to hear what your own sound is when you're not playing. That's why musicians often record themselves even when they are just practising. All you really need is a Walkman with an in-built microphone.

4. BUYING OR RENTING?

How much does a violin cost? Well, somewhere between a few hundred and a few million. But how much does a violin suitable for serious study cost, and what exactly are you paying for if you buy or rent a more expensive instrument?

Most children under twelve start on a rented violin, which can easily be exchanged for the next size up as they grow. Even if you are well above the age of twelve, renting a violin is a good way to start.

A better violin
It's easy to exchange a rented violin, not only easy for a bigger one, but also for a better one. What's more, maintenance is usually included in the rental fee, and of course it is in the rental firm's interest that repairs are done properly. After all, the violin remains their property.

Costs
You can rent a full-size violin from around £20/$10 a month, complete with bow and case. Insurance is often included too in the cost, but remember to check beforehand. Small violins are not necessarily cheaper to rent.

Hire purchase
Sometimes it's possible to buy the violin that you've been renting. If so, the rental fee, or part of it, will often be deducted from the price. That's another thing to ask about when you rent a violin.

Where?

There are special companies that rent out violins and other string instruments, but you can also try violin makers, music schools and music shops.

BUYING A VIOLIN?

Say you're looking for a new or secondhand full-size violin that you can learn to play on seriously, and enjoy for a good few years to come. How much will it cost you? Somewhere around £400/$700 and you'll need to add at least another £150/$200 for a simple bow and case.

Too cheap

Of course there are plenty of people who have had lasting enjoyment playing a much cheaper instrument. Then again, some cheap violins are barely playable without a lot of work being done on them. They might need a new bridge, a new fingerboard, or new tuning pegs because the old ones slip and have to be retuned every five minutes. Such an instrument can easily cost you an extra £70/$100 before you are even able to play it.

Better-looking, better-sounding

A higher-priced instrument has probably had more time and attention spent on it, has been made of higher quality materials, and more care has gone into matching the components to each other. The result is a better-looking, richer-sounding instrument, which may well be easier – and more rewarding – to play.

Ask the expert

The most important tip for buying your first instrument is to take someone who knows about violins with you. They will be able to tell you if a violin is better than its price might suggest, or the other way around. If you don't know a violinist you can take with you, try asking your teacher. And if you can't find anyone at all, at least buy one from someone who plays the instrument him or herself.

STUDENT VIOLINS AND VIRTUOSO VIOLINS

All kinds of names are used to classify violins: student

violins, orchestral violins, virtuoso soloist standard violins. What's what, and what do the names mean?

To begin with...

Sometimes you find violins classified as student violins, orchestral violins and concert violins. These names suggest that you should start off with the first, buy an orchestral violin once you are good enough to play in an orchestra, and move onto a concert violin to play solo concerts.

Problem

The trouble with these names is that they have no fixed meaning. For instance, some master violin makers build 'student violins' which sell for twice the price of 'concert violins' made in a large factory. So don't pay any attention to the names. The price will usually tell you more.

Handmade

'Handmade' is another word that can be misleading: you can buy low-cost factory-made violins that have been largely built by hand. It doesn't necessarily mean they are any good.

Hand-crafted

Alternatively, violins are sometimes classified as factory-made violins or hand-crafted violins. This description is much clearer. To buy a violin like this, made from start to finish by a real master craftsperson, you may have to pay £7000/$10,000, or even more. And there's a fair chance that you'll have to join a waiting list for delivery. It goes without saying that a master violin maker (sometimes called a *luthier*) does everything by hand, so that using the word 'handmade' here isn't really necessary.

Used violins

Everyone knows that violins made by the old masters can be incredibly expensive. Older factory-made violins can fetch a high price too, because many violinists believe that old instruments sound better, or more 'genuine'. Even so, a brand new instrument costing £500/$800 may be better than a violin made a century ago that costs almost twice the price.

Old factory-made violins

On the other hand: an old factory-made violin that has been played a lot and properly looked after is almost bound to be a good violin. Violins that don't sound good, aren't enjoyable to play or are hard to tune simply don't get played.

Violas and small violins

Violas tend to be more expensive than violins of the same standard. That's partly because they are bigger, but also because fewer of them are made. The same is true of bows, strings and cases. Small factory-made violins are not always cheaper than full-size violins.

A true story

This is a true story. A violinist goes to buy an expensive violin. He tries it out, examines it, plays it again and again until he is sure: this violin is the one for him. He's absolutely certain. But he doesn't buy it because, to his shock and surprise, he is told that the price is only in the low thousands – and he was actually looking for a violin that would cost at least twenty thousand. Yes, it really happened. In fact, it happens more often than you might think.

BUYING TIPS

What is the most important tip for when you're buying? Always go to someone who understands violins to buy your instrument. Then at least you'll come home with a playable instrument. As a general rule, the better an instrument sounds the more it will cost.

Where to buy?

Besides music shops, which tend to stock factory-made instruments in the main, you can buy from rental firms or makers, who may let you take a violin home with you to try it out for a while. Many makers also sell cheaper instruments, not just the expensive models of their own making.

Labels

You can also buy good secondhand violins through the classified ads in the paper or at auctions, if you know what to look for. A word of warning, though: there are thousands of violins around with labels bearing the name Stradivarius, or the names of other phenomenally expensive violin makers. Anyone can make a label. Making violins is harder.

Antonio Stradivarius Cremonenfis
Faciebar Anno 1999

Just about anyone can make a label

Appraisals

If you don't buy your instrument from a violin maker, take it to one for *appraisal* (or *valuation*). Violin makers can usually tell you exactly what a violin should cost. And they'll also point out anything that's wrong with it, and what it will cost to put it right. Ask what the appraisal will cost beforehand: it'll usually be one or two percent of the value of the violin. If that doesn't amount to much, you may have to pay a minimum charge instead.

Take your time

Take your time when you are buying a violin. After all, you want it to last you a long time. Only if you have really fallen in love with a violin should you buy it on the spot. Or maybe the next week – or after you've saved up enough money.

MORE AND MORE EXPENSIVE

Professional violinists and conservatory students often play instruments worth tens of thousands, and there are violins that cost more than a million. Why are they so expensive, and whoever can afford them?

Like paintings

Violins by famous makers like Stradivarius, Amati or Guarnerius don't command these high prices just because they are wonderful instruments, but also because they are at least three hundred years old.

Better?

Age doesn't make violins better, but it does make them more expensive. You can easily pay four times as much for an old instrument of high quality as for an equally good new violin.

Less famous, less expensive
The price of an old violin also depends on how well-known the maker is. A very good, rare German violin the same age as a Stradivarius may go for under £5000/$8000.

Reasonable?
When discussing old and expensive violins, you need to be wary of words like 'good', 'bad' or 'reasonable'. If one expert thinks you can get a 'reasonable violin' for two or three thousand, you can bet the next one will say that 'reasonable' starts at fifty thousand. Experts disagree on other matters too, some saying that a new violin needs a few years' playing in before it starts sounding good, while others say it takes fifteen minutes at the most.

Conservatory violins
Some conservatory students rent their expensive instruments, others are lucky enough to be able to buy them, and yet others complete their training with a decent violin that only cost a few thousand pounds or dollars. Some countries have institutions or foundations which lend expensive instruments to talented students and professionals.

5. A GOOD VIOLIN

To the beginner, all violins look much the same. This chapter explains the ways in which they can differ, and how the differences affect the sound. It also examines woods, varnishes, soundboxes, bridges and fine tuners as well as other aspects that will help you to get the very best violin you can afford.

Naturally the sound of a violin depends on how it was built, and on the quality of the wood. But the strings are important too, as are the bow, and the way the instrument is set up. You can read more about these last three subjects in chapters 6, 7 and 10.

Purely by ear
The first and largest part of this chapter is about how to judge a violin by looking at it, and how you can interpret these visual clues as a guide to the sound. If you prefer to choose a violin by its sound alone, then go straight to the testing and listening tips found on page 42 and following.

The colour
The ground coat and the dyes in the varnish give the violin its colour. Some violins are a very pale orange or even yellowish, others a very deep brown, and some are reddish or even purple. Violins in completely different colours, such as green or blue, are rare.

Shiny or matt
There are violins that are almost as shiny as glass. Some have a warmer glaze, while others have a matt finish. Some

violins look as though they have been dipped into a big pot of varnish, instead of being varnished with a brush or spray gun. If the varnish is too thick, the sound will suffer.

Types of varnish

Violin makers use all kinds of varnish. You need to be an expert to tell the difference. The old-fashioned oil varnish is strong, but it can take months to dry. Spirit-based varnish is used on violins in all price ranges. Synthetic varnishes are the hardest. Because it can be sprayed onto the instrument, factory-made violins are often finished with this type of varnish, as it saves time. Synthetic varnish is also strong and easy to clean.

Shading

Violins are not always the same colour all over. Older violins sometimes have lighter patches where they have been handled a great deal. These worn-out patches are sometimes imitated on newer violins. It's called *shading*, and it makes the violin look older than it really is.

Tiny cracks

On older violins, the varnish can be marked with *craquelure*, the thousands of tiny cracks you sometimes see on old paintings – but that effect, too, can be imitated. Alternatively, a dark dye may be applied to the grain to make the wood look older.

Aged to order

Some violins have been made to look older (*antiqued*) so that they sell for a higher price. If you have one built, you can of course ask the violin maker to do the same. Even minor damage and small repairs can be imitated.

Curl

The back and ribs of a violin sometimes have 'tiger stripes'. You usually only find such stripes or *curl*, also called *flamed* or *figured wood*, on more expensive violins. If you look, you'll notice the difference between broad and narrow, bold and light curl. The more obvious the curl, the more expensive the violin tends to be. You can see the effect best if you shine a light on the instrument and move it backwards and forwards. Often the two halves of the

back are very precisely *mirrored* or *book-matched*, so that the left and right sides look identical.

A mirrored, figured back

Fine scrolls

Most scrolls look like a perfect spiral, with sharply carved, smooth edges. Others seem to have been carved more clumsily. Does that mean that the violin is no good? Not necessarily. If you spot a 'clumsy' scroll, you might well be looking at a cheap factory violin but it could also be an old and expensive Italian model.

A perfect spiral and a clumsy job

Purfling

The purfling usually consists of three strips of wood, but sometimes there are more. This inlay is not just for decoration but also to protect the *plates* (the belly and back), making them less likely to crack if the body gets a knock. A tip: on very cheap violins, the purfling is sometimes not inlaid but painted onto the wood.

 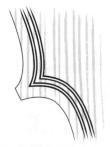

Purfling consists of three or more strips of wood.

THE BODY

The body of one violin may be a little higher or wider than that of the next, or a little slimmer at the *waist*, or the arching of the belly may be different. Violas can differ in size. Here is a short tour of the body.

(Not) all the same

Full-size violins are all pretty much the same size, down to fractions of an inch. But violas come in different sizes. The body of a small viola is about fifteen inches (39 cm) long, a big one about two inches (5 cm) longer.

Bigger violas

There are some beautiful small violas around, but a bigger model will usually sound a little larger and fuller. If you are looking for a smaller one, then it's a good idea to look for an instrument that's also a little wider and deeper; it's likely to sound more like a 'real' viola than a short model which is also narrow and shallow.

Slimmer violins

When it comes to violins, you need to learn to look carefully to see the differences between one body and the next. For instance, some bodies can be slightly stocky or 'fat', whilst other violins appear that little bit slimmer. This barely affects the sound, but it can mean that one violin will suit you better than another. For instance, if the body is narrow at the top, it may make it easier to reach the highest notes even if you have small hands.

Stradivarius

Many violins are still based on the instrument that Stradivarius designed around 1700, but names of other violin makers are used to indicate different models. Again, the differences are small, but they are well documented. A Stradivarius model is a little wider and has shorter *f*-holes than a Guarnerius model, for example.

The belly

The *belly*, *table* or *top* is the most important component of a violin. The strings make the belly vibrate, and it is these vibrations, more than anything else, which determine the sound of your violin.

Spruce

The belly is almost always made of solid spruce. The back is usually made of solid maple, a slightly heavier, denser wood. Some very cheap violins have a laminated back, made up of several thin layers of wood.

Fine grain

Violinists often prefer the belly to have a grain that is straight, even, and not too broad, getting gradually finer towards the centre of the violin. That doesn't make it an infallible guide though. Some violins with a wonderful grain don't have a good sound, and there are superb violins with an 'untidy' grain.

The arching

A flattish belly can provide a stronger, more powerful sound than a high-arched belly. The usual height of the 'ridge' of a violin's belly is somewhere between 0.6" and 0.7" (15–18mm). The back is a little flatter.

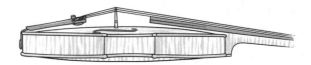

The back is a little flatter than the belly

The channel

A violin with a deep, broad channel will often have a softer sound than an instrument where this 'valley' along the edge is barely present.

Flowing lines

You can spend hours looking at violin archings. They all look similar, yet they are all slightly different. What is especially important is that the lines of the arch flow smoothly and there are no flat parts or odd angles. The arching should not be too high, too low or too narrow and sharp. The more often you look, the more you'll see.

Thick and thin

Some cheap violins have thicker bellies, because they can be made more quickly. If a violin belly is too thick, the instrument will usually sound a little thin. Master violin makers may measure the thickness of a belly to hundredths of an inch, so that they can give the violin exactly the sound they want.

Sides
The ribs of a full-size violin are a little over an inch (2.5 cm) high. A very shallow violin may sound harsh, and excessive depth may give a hollow sound. These differences in size may actually be very small. In violins, the ribs are virtually the same height all the way round. Violas are often deeper by the tailpiece than they are at the neck end.

Open and closed
Violin makers use animal glue for their instruments. Joins, or *seams*, fixed with animal glue can be loosened again if necessary, so that the body can easily be reopened if there is a need for an internal repair. This is difficult or impossible to do with other types of glue sometimes used for cheap factory violins.

NECK AND FINGERBOARD
The neck and fingerboard affect the playability and sound of a violin. They can also tell you something about how well-made it is.

Ebony
Fingerboards are almost always made of ebony, an extremely hard type of wood which is almost black in colour. The smoother and more even the fingerboard is, the easier playing on it will be. Cheap violins sometimes have fingerboards of soft, light-coloured wood, often painted black to make it look like ebony. You may be able to recognize such a fingerboard by lighter patches on the sides, or even by spotting bits the painter has missed. After years of use, even the hardest fingerboard will wear. There's more about this subject in chapter 10, *Violin Maintenance*.

Fat fingers
The grooves in the nut, at the top of the fingerboard, determine how the strings are spaced and how high they rise above the fingerboard at that point. Nuts can be

replaced. If you have fat fingers, you may prefer a nut with grooves set a little further apart – and vice versa.

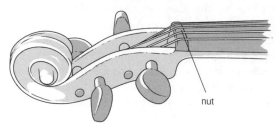

nut

The nut can be replaced

Feel

Necks are always lighter in colour – a dark neck would soon show up all the worn patches. On more expensive violins, the wood is usually not varnished but protected with a little oil. Feel if the curve of the neck lies nicely in your hand and that there are no odd pits or bumps.

Curved fingerboard

If you look from the side you will see that the fingerboard has a very slight concave curve. If it were completely flat, the strings might vibrate against it.

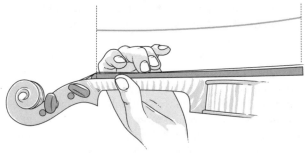

The fingerboard is always very slightly curved

Straight

The neck and the fingerboard must be absolutely straight throughout their length, and set exactly in the centre line of the violin. They should not curve slightly to the left or the right. Nor should it look as though someone has tried to wrench the instrument out of shape. So always take a good look along the neck from the scroll towards the bridge.

In the centre

Another tip for examining violins: hold the violin with the tailpiece towards you and first check that the bridge is set exactly in the centre, between the inner nicks of the *f*-holes. If it is, check that the strings run exactly straight along the fingerboard.

Tilting downwards

Looking from the side, you'll see that the neck has a slight downwards tilt. Before 1800, this was not the case. In those days, the neck and the side of the body were at a 90-degree angle to each other, and as a result the strings pressed down less hard on the bridge. That's why early violins sound softer. A smaller neck angle increases the pressure on the bridge, making the sound bigger and louder – more radiant, some people say.

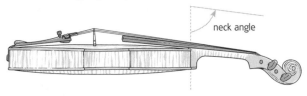

neck angle

A smaller neck angle gives a bigger sound

ACTION

The *action* is the distance between the strings and the fingerboard. Having the strings a long way above the fingerboard (a high action) makes playing harder. If they are too low (low action), they may touch the fingerboard when they vibrate and produce an unpleasant buzz. In between, it's largely a matter of taste. A higher action can give your instrument a slightly clearer or more powerful sound.

How high?

At the nut, the strings should lie just above the fingerboard. At the other end of the fingerboard, the distance between the fingerboard and the strings is a lot greater. At this point the thicker strings are always slightly higher above the fingerboard than the thin ones, because they need more room to move. The E-string usually has an action of around 0.12" (3mm), while the G-string will be about 0.16" to 0.20" (4–5mm) above the fingerboard. Gut strings need a higher action, steel strings a lower one.

Too high

If you have a new violin which has not yet been properly set up, the action may well be on the high side. This will make playing hard work. Something can be done about that by fitting a lower bridge and a lower nut.

THE BRIDGE

The bridge matters not just because it keeps the strings at the right height, but also for its effect on the sound of the instrument.

Straight

A bridge is slanted at the front and straight at the back. The back must be exactly vertical to the belly, and the feet of the bridge must be placed exactly between the inner nicks of the *f*-holes.

Speckled wood

Some bridges look completely featureless, while others may be highly speckled. In itself this difference tells you nothing about the quality of the wood, as either type may be used for cheap or expensive bridges alike. A good, straight grain is more important.

A speckled bridge

Bridges and sound

Of course you're not going to weigh a bridge when you're choosing a violin, but it's worth knowing that a heavy bridge can muffle the sound slightly, just like a mute (see page 69). If you have a light bridge, the sound may become thin, weak or unfocused.

The hardness of the wood also plays a role. A bridge made of harder wood increases the volume and contributes to a stronger, more brilliant tone.

Models

Bridges come in different models, but you'll need to look very carefully to tell them apart. A violin maker does see those differences, and he or she should be the one to set a new bridge on your violin if you need it. A bridge must always be tailor-made – even if it has moveable feet which automatically adjust to the arch of the belly.

A rare adjustable bridge with moveable feet

Not too deep

The longer an instrument has been played, the deeper the strings will have cut into the bridge. If the grooves are too deep the strings will be muffled and harder to tune, and the action will decrease. Ideally the grooves will be just deep enough for two-thirds of the thickness of each string to be proud of the bridge.

Cutting string

The E-string, which is about 0.01" (0.25 mm) thick, is the one most likely to cut into your bridge. That's why some bridges have a piece of bone or hardwood set into them at this point. A plastic sleeve or a piece of vellum (parchment) can also help (see page 52).

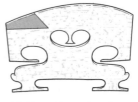

A bridge with an ebony inset

Two at once

The top of the bridge has almost the same curve as the top of the fingerboard. The bridge is at its highest in the middle and its lowest by the thinnest string. When you are just starting, it's a good idea to have a bridge with a steep curve: this makes it less likely that you will bow two strings at once.

Collapsed bridges

In time, nearly all bridges collapse slightly under the pressure of the strings. A violin will only produce its best sound with a straight bridge – so have your bridge replaced in good time.

High bridges

Most bridges are between 0.12 and 0.14 inches (31–35 mm) high at their topmost point. Too high a bridge can produce a slightly hollow sound, although a high bridge is sometimes used to compensate for a very small neck angle.

THE SOUNDPOST

Inside the body, slightly behind the bridge, is the sound-post. This thin round stick is not just there for strength; it also has a lot to do with the sound. That's why the French call it *l'âme*, or the soul of the violin.

Precision

The soundpost must be straight. It needs to be long enough to be firmly wedged into position, but not so long that it pushes the belly and back apart. Exactly where it sits is critical too, with a 20th of an inch (1mm) making a difference to the sound.

Adjustment

A violin maker can adjust the sound of a violin by moving the soundpost a fraction, making the instrument sound slightly less shrill, or a little clearer. In addition, if one string sounds louder or softer than the others the maker can do something about it by moving the soundpost – or by using different strings, but that's something dealt with in chapter 6.

TUNING

You can tune a violin by means of the wooden tuning pegs at the top. In many cases, you'll use the fine tuners in the tailpiece as well, or instead. Both pegs and fine tuners come in different types and sizes.

Hardwood

Pegs get thicker towards the knob; this shape prevents them from twisting loose by themselves. They are usually made of ebony. This type of wood is also used for tail-pieces and chin rests, although rosewood and boxwood are popular too. Rosewood is reddish-brown in colour; boxwood is usually yellowish.

Softwood

Very cheap violins sometimes have pegs made out of soft-wood. Why is hardwood a better choice? It's because the strings wear grooves into softwood pegs more quickly, and when a string is jammed in a groove it is more likely to break.

A good fit

Tuning pegs must turn easily, but they must not slip. Cheap violins are often hard to tune or go out of tune quickly because the pegs are poor quality or don't fit properly.

Parisian eyes

Pegs come in a surprising variety of forms, for instance in the form of an inverted heart, with a ball on top, or they may be decorated, perhaps with a *Parisian eye*: a small, mother-of-pearl circle with a metal ring around it. A single mother-of-pearl circle is simply called an *eye* or an *eyelet*.

basic peg   Parisian eye   ball   inverted heart

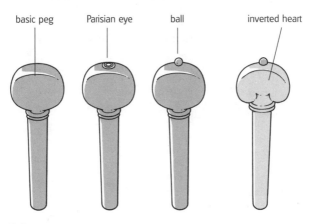

Tuning pegs

Fine tuners

If you use steel strings then *fine tuners* (also called *tuning adjusters*, *string tuners* and *string adjusters*) are indispensable. They're also very convenient if you use synthetic strings. Less expensive violins may have four fine tuners built into the tailpiece, but you can also buy them separately. Many violinists combine three gut strings with a single steel string (high E), which will then be the only string to have a fine tuner.

Short or long

Fine tuners come in different shapes and sizes. Longer models stick out a little way, while short ones can be actually built into the tailpiece or fixed right by its end. Usually, you won't see much of them besides the screw heads. Makers of short fine tuners include Hill, Uni and Piccolo.

Easier

Long fine tuners make tuning a little easier than the short ones since less strength is needed to operate them. It's easier to fit new strings as well. If the tailpiece lies very close to the belly, perhaps because the belly has a high arch, you are better off with short fine tuners: long fine tuners may damage the wood if turned too far.

(Non)sense

Some violinists prefer short fine tuners because long ones reduce the string length between bridge and tailpiece, and they think this affects the sound for the worse. There are at least as many others who say that it is nonsense – so this is something you may want to test for yourself.

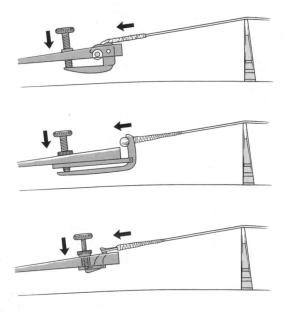

An in-built fine tuner (top), long and short fine tuners

Loop or ball

Most strings have a ball at one end, which fits inside the fine tuner. Steel E strings come with either a ball or a loop, the loop end strings requiring a different type of fine tuner. Some fine tuners, though, can handle both loop and ball ends. There are also special fine tuners for gut strings. Most types cost £1–3/$2–5 each.

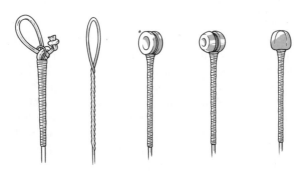

Some strings have a loop, others a ball end

TAILPIECE

Tailpieces may be made of wood, metal or plastic, may be plain or decorated, and may or may not have fine tuners built in. The tailpiece, too, influences the sound of your instrument.

Slim or angular

There is great variety of tailpieces available, especially wooden ones. Two typical examples are the French model, with a very slim upper part, or the Hill model, named after a British manufacturer, with elegant lines and an angular end.

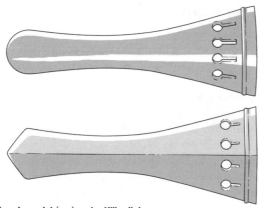

A French model (top) and a Hill tailpiece

Golden fret

If you have gold-coloured fine tuners you might want the *fret* (the little ridge which the strings run over) to be the same colour rather than the usual black. Tailpieces can have other decorations, such as a Parisian eye, or inlays.

The sound

The tailpiece has roughly the same effect on the sound of the violin as the bridge does and a heavy tailpiece can muffle the sound slightly. A lighter tailpiece will give a clearer sound, but you might find that the sound loses some of its foundation and strength, just as when a bridge is too light. Of course, the difference won't be that huge unless you have a heavy tailpiece which is too close to the bridge (see page 93) and has four big, long fine tuners in it. All that extra weight near the bridge will make the violin sound noticeably duller. Another thing to check is that the strings run parallel between the bridge and the tailpiece. If not, the tailpiece is too narrow or too wide for the violin.

Violas

Because violas differ in size so do viola tailpieces. Sometimes a small viola will have a violin tailpiece fitted, but this will usually be too small, and the length of the strings between bridge and tailpiece will be too great. The right tailpiece for the instrument would certainly improve the sound. Viola tailpieces often have the size of the viola they are made for marked on the bottom.

TIPS ON TESTING

If you try ten violins in a row, you'll have forgotten what the first one sounded like by the time you try the last. The tips given below will make it easier to make comparisons.

Take your own along

If you already have a violin, take it with you when you go to choose another instrument, as it will give you a reference point when comparing sounds. If you have your own bow, take that with you too. Otherwise, use the best bow available in the shop. Using a good bow will give you a better idea about what the various instruments are capable of.

Someone else

If you don't play yet or have only just started, you won't know whether an instrument has a poor sound, or whether it's just you. So why not ask someone who does play to demonstrate the different violins to you? That someone could be the person selling or renting out the instrument.

By ear

If you ask someone else to play, you can also hear how the violin sounds from a distance. The sound will be quite different compared to having it right by your ear. Another tip: if you simply can't choose between a few violins, turn around so you don't know which violin is being played. You won't know the price, the colour, the finish or the age, so you'll end up choosing by the sound alone. Sometimes a musician doing it this way will end up with a much cheaper instrument than they planned – although it may be the other way round.

Suggestion

Instead of choosing lots and lots of violins, you can ask the salesperson or the person renting you the instrument to suggest different violins in the price range you are looking for. Listening is all about comparisons. If you thought the first one was too bright, ask for a violin with a more subdued tone. Or ask to try two very different violins. Listen to a crystal-clear violin, then a rich, warm one, and then continue your search from there.

Two out of three

First make a rough selection of the instruments you like on first hearing. Take three of them, and compare them with one another. Remember the one you like best, and replace the one you like least by another violin from your selection. Then choose the best one again. And so on.

Play something simple

If you have a lot of violins to choose from it's a good idea to only play a short passage on each one. Play something simple, so that you only need to pay attention to the violin, and not to the notes. Even a simple scale will do. Only when you have narrowed the choice down to a few violins and are ready to make a final decision should you play longer pieces, so that you can get to know the instruments better.

String by string

You can also compare violins string by string or note by note. How does the open E-string sound? Do all four strings sound equally loud, and how do the strings sound in the highest positions? How do they sound when you pluck them, or when you play long notes?

The same

The instruments need to be tuned properly, and to the same pitch. Otherwise, one violin might sound a little warmer than the others, for instance, just because it is tuned a bit lower. For similar reasons, you should ideally compare instruments fitted with the same type of strings – otherwise you will be comparing strings instead of violins.

LISTENING TIPS

Of course, it's impossible to put into words how different violins sound, at least words that everyone agrees on. But the following tips will make listening a lot easier.

Volume and projection

Some violins will always sound very soft or weak, however energetically you play them. If you play in an orchestra your sound will get lost. Other violins can be heard at a fair distance, even if you play very softly. A violin like that has good *projection*.

Evenness

The E-string is not only tuned higher than the other strings, but it has a different tone. If you play the same E note first on the open E-string, then on the stopped A-string and then on the stopped D-string, you'll hear the same note sound very different each time. This is unavoidable, of course. All the same, a violin should have an even sound: the differences between strings must not be too big.

Response

A violin should have a good response. That means it sounds good and speaks immediately even when you play very softly. If not, the instrument will make playing and learning how to play very hard, because you really have to work for each note. A slow response may also be the fault of the strings (heavier ones respond slower), or the bow – or the player.

Dynamics and colour

A violin needs to produce a wide range of dynamics, from soft to very loud. If it doesn't do this, its performance will always be a bit shallow. The instrument should also be able to produce different tone colours or *timbres*. One example: if you bow the string a little closer to the fingerboard it should sound noticeably rounder than when you play near the bridge – and it should sound good both ways.

Preference

Other than that, sound is a matter of personal preference. When two people listen to the same violin, they often use very different words to describe what they hear. What one person describes as 'harsh' another may find 'bright'; what one calls 'warm' another may call 'woolly', and so on. They are hearing the same thing but they have different tastes – or at least different ways of describing sounds.

Oo or ee

Instead of words, you can use sounds to describe what you like, or to explain the kind of violin you are looking for. For instance, violinists sometimes talk about violins which have a lot of 'oo' (a dark, warm sound) or, alternatively, a lot of 'ee' (a bright, radiant sound). If there's too much oo, the sound is dull. If there's too much ee, it's too harsh. And of course, there are all the shades in between.

The same

A violin may sound nasal, hollow, thin or dull. Although they're difficult to define exactly, everyone has more or less the same idea of what the words mean. And no one wants a violin with a sound like that.

More of everything

The better an instrument is, the richer it sounds. Richer means that there is more of everything. High and low, warm and bright, subdued and sharp, loud and soft…

USED VIOLINS

If you're buying a secondhand violin you'll need to watch out for the same things as with a brand new one. But of course there are a few points that demand extra attention.

Repairs

First of all: no matter what's broken, a violin can practically always be fixed. Of course, if you decide to buy an instrument that needs work done on it you do need to know how much it's going to cost first. Some types of damage are easy to see, other kinds only an expert will spot. If in doubt, take a violin for appraisal first (see also page 24).

Major damage: cracks near the soundpost and bass-bar

What to watch out for

- **Worn varnish**. One important place to check is where your left hand touches **the body**. If the varnish has completely gone, you need to do something about it.
- After repairs, **the varnish** is usually touched up. Make sure this *retouche* has been done properly.
- Check **the edges**: this is often where the **worst damage** is. Repairing the edges can easily cost £300/$500.
- Cracks in the plates always run lengthways. Cracks by **the soundpost and the bass-bar** are often hard to see and even harder to repair.
- Other places to check for cracks include the shoulder of the **neck and the cheeks** (sides) of the pegbox near the pegs.
- If **the tuning pegs** are pushed very far into the pegbox, the pegs may need replacing and the holes made smaller – and that's quite an expensive job (see page 85).
- Glue can come loose, along the edges, or *seams*, of the plates for instance, at the join in the centre of the back, or by the shoulder of the neck. Tap a violin very softly with a knuckle: this can sometimes help you discover **loose seams**.

- Check the **arching of the belly**. Sometimes the pressure of the strings makes the belly a little flatter near the bass-bar, or a little higher by the soundpost.

Cracks in the cheeks and the shoulder of the neck

Unwelcome guests

To end this chapter, a few words about woodworm. These tiny grubs burrow into wood leaving narrow tunnels. This can be a very serious problem, especially if they have been at work in the plates. Sometimes you can even see the tunnels. You won't find woodworm if a violin has been played regularly: woodworm don't like music. If you want to know whether they are still around, lay the instrument on a piece of black cardboard overnight. If there is sawdust on the cardboard the next day, you have unwelcome guests.

6. GOOD STRINGS

For hundreds of years all violin strings were made of gut. These days you can buy steel strings and synthetic strings as well, and both types come in many different varieties. Each type of string produces a different sound, some strings are easier to play on than others, and some strings suit one violin better than another.

Violin strings can last a long time – up to a year, or even longer. It does help if they are fitted properly and kept clean. For more guidance on how to keep your strings in good condition, go to chapter 10, *Violin Maintenance*.

Gut, steel, synthetic

To begin with, there are three main types of strings. Gut strings were the earliest kind, followed by steel strings, with a clearer sound. Synthetic strings didn't appear until the 1950s, but they are now very widely used.

A profound effect

Strings can have a profound effect on the sound of your violin, and on how easy it is to play. Indeed, the difference in the sound produced by cheap and expensive strings can be much greater than that between two differently priced violins. The same is true for steel and gut strings.

Expensive

Here's a tip: don't always buy the same strings. Try some really expensive strings too, even on a less expensive violin. You may well find that only then will your instrument show you everything it is capable of.

Windings

Most strings are wound with an ultrathin metal ribbon (the *winding*). Because of this winding the string itself can be fairly thin, so that it responds easily while still being able to produce a deep enough sound. How a string sounds depends on the material the core is made from, but also on the winding. One string is practically never wound: the E-string.

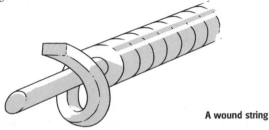

A wound string

Hard and soft

Finally, there is also a difference between 'hard' and 'soft' strings, or strings with a higher or lower tension, and between thicker and thinner strings. This chapter tells you what you need to know about these important differences. There's one thing to note first of all: strings for violas are always a little more expensive. The prices mentioned are for violin strings in sets of four, so violists can expect to pay a little more. If you buy strings individually rather than as a set, the thickest string will normally cost two to three times more than the thinnest.

GUT STRINGS

The first violins had gut strings, and there are still violinists who feel that the instrument sounds best with this type of strings – especially when playing music written in the days when these were the only strings available. Gut strings have a softer, richer sound that only develops fully once the strings have been played in, which takes a few hours. They also stretch a fair bit when new, which means you'll have to retune them quite often at first.

Expense

Gut strings don't last that long and are quite expensive. A set of four will easily cost £30/$50 or more.

Steel E

You don't often find gut E-strings, because they are very prone to breaking. Even so, they are still used by some violinists, particularly those who specialize in performing Baroque music from the seventeenth and early eighteenth centuries, and seek to attain an authentic sound. Most violinists use a steel E-string.

Wound E or plain E

A steel E-string may be wound, but it is usually a single thin steel wire, called a *plain string*. A plain string sounds a little clearer than a wound one.

STEEL STRINGS

If you use a complete set of steel strings, the instrument will produce a much clearer and brighter sound than with a set of gut strings. Steel strings are more reliable and they last a relatively long time, typically a year or more. Very cheap violins often have steel strings, because steel sets are available from around £11.50/$15. More expensive steel strings cost up to three or four times as much.

Bright

Because of their bright tone, steel strings sound especially good on violins with a slightly subdued sound. They are also popular with violinists who need a lot of volume. Most steel strings have a core of several very thin steel wires. Strings with a single, thicker steel wire inside give extra tone and there are also steel strings which have been specially treated to sound a little warmer.

Spare strings

Steel strings have other advantages. They don't need playing in, and they don't require constant retuning when new. They sound good immediately. For this reason, they also make good spares for performance. If a string breaks you can just fit a new one and carry on playing.

The E

Steel E-strings vary more than the others, and are priced at £1–8/$1–15. They may be wound or plain (the other steel strings are always wound) and steel E-strings can also differ in thickness, resilience and what they are made of. Since ordinary steel easily discolours and goes out of tune in the process some musicians prefer a chrome-steel string or a string plated with silver, gold or another material. This ultra thin finish both protects the steel and gives a slightly warmer sound.

SYNTHETIC STRINGS

Synthetic strings are very widely used, by beginners and professional string players alike. The sound resembles that of gut strings, but they are more reliable, easier to play and cheaper – most sets cost £20–35/$35–50.

Although every make and series has its own particular sound, as a general rule they are warmer and less hard and bright than steel strings. They don't usually last quite as long.

Playing in

Like gut strings, some synthetic strings only start to sound their best after a few hours' playing. When brand-new they sometimes sound a little raw, bold or hard. Violinists often use a steel E-string with a set of synthetic strings.

WINDINGS

To make sure that the strings of a set fit together as well as possible, manufacturers often use different windings. Silver for the G-string, for instance, because this makes it sound a little clearer, but aluminium for the D and A to make them sound a bit fuller.

Violas

You'll come across all kinds of combinations for violas too. Two with silver windings and two with aluminium, perhaps, going from low to high. Or maybe silver, chrome and two aluminium.

Steel wound

All the strings in a steel set will often have the same winding. Steel sets with nickel or aluminium windings sound a little softer, sweeter or warmer than steel strings with a chrome-steel winding.

More choices

Many more materials may be used to wind strings, including copper, titanium, tungsten or silver alloyed with gold or aluminium. If you are after a specific sound a good salesperson or maker will be able to help you with your choice. But if you really want to be sure, you'll need to try out different strings yourself. The same is true when you want to choose between thicker and thinner strings, or between louder and softer sounding strings.

LOUD OR SOFT

Synthetic and steel strings often come in several varieties: *dolce* (soft), *medium* and *forte* (strong) are common terms. You may also see German descriptions like *weich* and *stark*.

Lower tension

Softer-sounding strings have a lower tension than louder strings. Some string manufacturers describe their strings by the tension: you can buy *low*, *medium* and *high tension strings*. Strings with a higher tension take a little more effort to play and respond less quickly, but in return you get more volume. Medium strings are the most commonly used.

Colours

To indicate the tension of strings manufacturers use coloured thread at one end or the other. The same strings will have a different coloured thread at the other end to indicate which of the four strings of the set is which: each one has its own colour. Unfortunately these codes are not uniform, so the same colour may mean one thing for one make and something else for the next. Some brands have the colours that indicate the type of strings on the side of the scroll, while others do it the other way around.

Mixed up

A tip: if the strings on a violin are of the same make and series, you will see four different colours (the different strings) at one end, and only one colour (the colour of the series) at the other. If this is not the case, there's a fair chance that strings of different makes or tensions have been mixed together. If they all sound good, there's no problem. If you want to know which strings are fitted to your instrument, ask an expert. They can usually tell from the colour codes.

Thick or thin

With gut strings, you can choose among up to seven different thicknesses for one string. Thicker strings are harder work to play, they sound 'fatter', harder and clearer, and they don't respond as readily as thinner strings. If you want to know exactly how thick a gut string is in millimetres, divide the size (or *gauge*) by twenty: a size 14 string is 14/20 of an inch or 0.7mm thick. You can also calculate the gauge in inches: to do so, divide the gauge by five thousand (5080 if you want absolute precision).

Strong strings on a light instrument

If you put higher tension strings on your instrument it may happen that your strings end up further from the fingerboard – or closer if you fit lower tension strings. A violin maker will adjust the action if necessary. One way is to fit a different bridge (see page 93). Do bear in mind that instruments of lighter build are not built for the high tension of forte strings.

MORE STRING THINGS

Here a few final tips about balls and loops, and about how long you can expect strings to last, plastic sleeves and brands.

Ball or loop

As discussed on page 38, steel E-strings come with either a loop or a ball at the end that is attached to the fine tuner. Check your fine tuner to see which type you need.

Write it down

If you are putting new strings on your violin, write down the type you are using. That way you'll be able to buy the same type if you like them, or avoid them if you don't. You can note down the details of your strings on page 121 of this book.

How long

How long your strings last depends on many things: how often you play, of course, but also on the core material of the strings and the type of winding, on how well you keep your strings clean, and on the type of sweat you have. Most windings react badly to 'acid fingers'. You'll find more tips in chapter 10, where you'll also learn how to tell when it's time to replace one or more of your strings.

Sleeves

Strings often come with little plastic sleeves around them. These prevent the strings from cutting into the bridge, and stop the bridge damaging the strings. Most of the sleeve should be towards the tail end of the instrument; otherwise it will muffle the sound too much. That said, a little muffling may actually be desirable with a steel E-string, which in any case is the string most likely to cut into the bridge. Muffling makes the sound a little sweeter and less shrill. You can also buy rubber *tone filters* with the same effect. (Sometimes they are included for free.) A small piece of rubber tubing under the string does the same job.

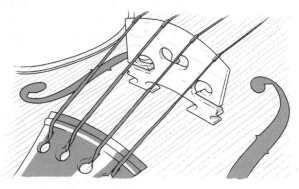

Plastic sleeves around the strings

Strings for children's violins

You can buy special, shorter strings (*fractional sizes*) for small violins and violas.

The makes

Just about every make of violin strings offers a number of different series. You can buy steel strings by D'Addario (Helicore), Pirastro (Chromcor) and Thomastik (Spirocore), for instance, and the same brands also make synthetic strings, such as the D'Addario Pro Arte, the Pirastro Tonica and the Thomastik Dominant. Pirastro has a huge range of gut strings, such as the Eudoxa and the expensive Oliv. Other well-known brands are Corelli, Kaplan and Jargar.

Choosing yourself

And finally: some violinists prefer to put together their own sets of strings. An E and an A of chrome or aluminium, perhaps, and a D or a G with a silver or chrome winding. Or a set made up of various materials, with gut, wound steel and plain steel from low to high. In this way you can pick exactly the right strings for your violin and adjust its sound to the way you play.

7. A GOOD BOW

You'll only get the very best from your violin if you have a good bow. What counts as a good bow partly depends on how you play, but also on your violin itself and on the sound you are looking for. This is a chapter about pernambuco and Brazil wood, frogs, ferrules, weight and balance, and rosin.

Bows are classified by their quality, just like violins. There are student bows, orchestral bows and high quality 'virtuoso' bows. And just as with violins, these terms don't mean much because everyone uses them differently.

The wood
What's much more important is the wood the stick is made from. Cheaper bows are almost always made of Brazil wood, and most violinists start out with this type of bow. The more expensive bows are usually made of pernambuco (sometimes spelled fernambuco), a slightly reddish type of wood. Pernambuco bows can last for over a century and still play as well as when they were new.

Overlap
For around £150/$200 you can buy one of the most expensive Brazil wood bows or a cheap pernambuco bow. If two bows cost the same, choose the one that best suits your needs, whichever type of wood it's made from.

Mounting
The *mounting* refers to the metal parts of the bow, such as the adjuster, the *back-plate* of the frog, and the *D-ring* or

ferrule, where the ribbon enters the frog. The material used for the mountings on pernambuco bows is a good clue to their price and quality.

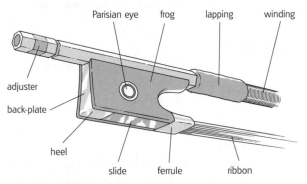

A fully-lined frog

Silver, gold and nickel silver
Bows with a silver mounting start at around £275/$350. You can buy a bow with gold mounting from around £1250/$2000. Cheaper pernambuco bows have mountings of nickel silver, also known as German silver or alpaca, an alloy which does not contain a drop of silver.

Fully-lined
The frog in the picture above is a *fully-lined* frog. A *half-lined* frog does not have a back plate behind the slide or extending underneath it.

Synthetic materials
The stick may be made of a synthetic material or carbon fibre. The cheapest models, costing around £30/$50 upwards, are designed mainly for children: they can take a knock and don't need much attention. But synthetic bows for professional violinists are also available, and they can cost several thousands.

Children's bows
Of course, you can also find smaller bows intended for smaller hands. They are usually made of Brazil wood.

Viola bows
Since violas are larger, you might expect viola bows to be

longer – but they're not. In fact, viola bows are often about 0.2 inches (5mm) shorter than violin bows. Even so, they are heavier, because a light violin bow doesn't have the weight to get the strings of a viola to vibrate enough.

CLOSE UP

Of course, there is more to a bow than the type of wood used and the mounting. The shape of the stick makes a difference to the sound, and the decorations on and around the frog make a difference to the look.

Eight-sided or round

The *stick*, which gets gradually thinner from the frog to the head, can be round or octagonal (eight-sided) – rather like a fishing rod. Some violinists prefer octagonal sticks, which may be a little stiffer or more stable than round sticks, but it's very much a personal matter. An octagonal stick is usually more expensive than a round version of the same stick: not because it's necessarily superior, but because it takes more work to make one.

Frog

The frog, named after a similarly shaped part of a horse's hoof, is usually made of ebony. Cheap sticks sometimes have a frog made of a synthetic material. The *slide*, at the bottom of the frog, usually has a mother-of-pearl finish. The frog itself is often decorated with dots or Parisian eyes, and some models are intricately carved and decorated.

Adjuster

The adjuster is often inlaid. Expensive sticks often have costlier decorations, sometimes with a circle of mother-of-pearl on each side of the octagonal adjuster.

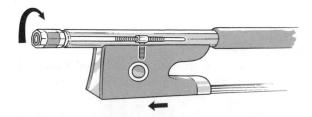

This is how you move the frog: by turning the adjuster.

Branding
The make of bow or maker's name is often branded into the wood of the stick, just above the frog.

Lapping
The lapping or thumb grip gives you more grip on the bow. It may be a little thinner on one stick than another, and occasionally it has tiny 'ventilation holes'. Cheaper bows may use synthetic leather though it may feel a little sticky. If the lapping is too thin or too thick it can easily be replaced.

Winding
There is often a separate winding next to the lapping, usually of silver wire. The synthetic windings in one or two colours you sometimes come across are imitation baleen (whalebone). The use of real baleen has been banned.

Head
The protective *face* at the other end of the stick was often made of ivory in the past. Contemporary bow makers use plastic, metal or bone.

Hair
The ribbon consists of one hundred and fifty or more horse-tail hairs. Just like human hair, horsehair is not completely smooth: it has tiny scales which are invisible to the naked eye. These scales provide a good grip for the violin rosin. Synthetic hair is only used on cheap bows.

THE BEST BOW
How much should a bow cost, and which type is the best? There are no straightforward answers to either of these questions. The most important tip is this: buy a bow from an expert. The next section tells you what to look out for.

Price
Some violinists say your bow should cost as much as your violin. Others say half or a quarter as much. So that's not much help. The best advice is to buy the bow you feel most comfortable with, which gets as close as possible to the sound you want from your violin, and which you can afford.

Suitability

Which bow would suit you best? Well, it depends on the way you play, but also on how and where you hold it and the length of your arm. Most of all, a bow has to suit your violin and the strings you use.

Better – or just expensive?

Just as with violins, expense does not guarantee quality, and an antique bow will often cost a lot more than an equally good new one. With luck, you can find a splendid bow for a bargain price. Many top violinists have at least one 'cheap' bow in their collection because it's perfect for certain pieces of music.

Suiting the music

In other words, the bow should suit the style of music you play. Violinists often use one bow for earlier music, say from before 1800, and another for more recent compositions. Typically, they will own a variety of bows. Some bows are better for fast, energetic, loud music, whereas other bows are better for when you need to play softly.

CHOOSING BOWS

After you've tried out ten bows in a row, you'll have forgotten what the first one was like. It's often easier if you start with two or three bows. Choose the best, then compare it with another. Start by playing short, simple pieces, or simply scales, and play longer pieces when you have narrowed down the choice.

What to play

Of course, the best test for any bow is to play the music you intend to use it for. Try out all the bowing styles you know. Play slowly, fast, loud and soft, and keep on listening and feeling how the bow performs. Some bows will fit the way that you as an individual play better than others.

Sound

Each bow is different. It may sound clear or warm, dark or light, full or thin, elegant or coarse. Playing long notes is the best way to hear the differences. Again, some bows sound louder than others. Cheaper factory-made bows have fewer variations than expensive bows, but they have them nonetheless. In fact, there are even small differences between two bows of the same type produced by the same factory or craftsperson.

Curved

A bow should be curved so that the ribbon, when slack, just touches the stick. If the stick is more curved than that, the ribbon may touch it when playing. Such a bow may also feel a little restless – a bit jumpy, you might say. On the other hand, too straight a bow may be a little sluggish. Looking on the bright side, you could also say that a curved bow is good for *spiccato* (lightly bouncing the bow off the strings) and a fairly straight bow for fine, long notes. But then, a really good bow should allow you to play anything.

Springy

If you take a bow by both ends and bend it carefully, you can feel how elastic or springy it is. A very supple bow can make it difficult to play fast pieces, but it may have a better tone than a stiffer bow. It may be generally easier to play with a stiffer bow, but making a good, long tone may become trickier. Once again: with a good bow you should be able to play anything.

Weight

A full-size bow usually weighs between 2 and 2.3 ounces (56–65 grams). The heavier it is, the more volume you can produce with it. If your bow is too light, it won't make the strings vibrate enough and you won't produce much sound at all. Some violinists claim that even a gram makes a difference between the feel of two bows.

Balance

The heavier a bow is at the head end, the heavier it will feel as a whole. Make sure the ribbon is slack and hold the bow between your thumb and forefinger about ten inches (25cm) from the end of the stick itself (not including the adjuster). If the head dips, the balance of your bow is quite far forwards.

Top-heavy

A top-heavy stick like this may well be easier to control,

whereas a stick with the weight further back feels lighter, but needs more guidance.

Response

With some bows, the tone builds up very gently and gradually, and with others the strings respond much more quickly and precisely. To check the response of a bow, play lots of short notes on the lowest strings. Most violinists like to have a bow with an even response, in other words, a bow that produces the same response from the strings in the middle, near the head and near the frog.

A straight line

Another tip: look along the back of the bow, from the frog, to check that it is straight. The bow must not look as though someone has tried to wring it out.

Secondhand bows

A few tips if you're planning to buy a used bow.

- If the ribbon is overstretched, a bow will feel very floppy when you play. The solution is simple: have the bow rehaired (see page 86).
- Another problem with an overstretched ribbon is that the frog needs to be shifted very far back to make the ribbon taut enough, and this changes the balance of the stick.
- A bow can lose some of its curve over the years. Sometimes bows can be worked back into shape, but make sure your bow is worth it before spending the money.
- What Stradivarius is to the violin, Tourte is to the bow. Tourte was a French bow maker who died in 1835. You may occasionally come across his name on a bow. It probably won't be a real Tourte, because the real ones fetch more than £35,000/$50,000.

Makes

A few well-known bow makes are Dörfler, Höfner, Paesold and Werner from Germany, and Ary-France, Roger, Spiccato and Student Arpège from France. Low-cost synthetic bows are made by Schaller, Glasser and other companies. There are also dozens of small bow workshops, especially in Germany, which make bows costing from around £125/

$200. Bows by independent makers, who work alone, start at around £700/$1000. The very cheapest bows often don't have a brand name.

ROSIN

Without rosin, the ribbon would simply glide across your strings in silence, so you rub it with rosin to help it 'bite'. Which rosin should you use? There are many different types, and even more theories on the subject.

The same

Most violinists stick with the same rosin for years. Still, trying out another type or brand can't hurt. Here are some guidelines.

Hard and sticky

Rosin comes wrapped in a cloth or in a box so you don't get it on your fingers. It's not only sticky, but also quite hard. Rosin will easily last you a year or longer, unless you drop it: it's quite brittle, so there's a good chance it'll break.

Light and dark

Many rosins are available in two colours, costing the same: a light, honey colour, and a darker colour, almost like liquorice. If there is no other information given, you can assume that it really is only the colour which is different. And when you start playing and the rosin turns to powder, both types end up the same colour: white.

Rosin is sold in cloths and boxes, rectangular or round blocks, and in different colours.

Harder and softer

Rosins vary in hardness. The rosin of one brand may be harder than that of another, and some brands sell rosin in various hardnesses. You may be able to feel the difference between the softer and harder types by pressing your nail into them.

Which rosin

Choosing the best rosin is a much discussed subject but unfortunately the experts disagree wildly. The commonest opinions are that softer rosin makes your strings respond better, but because it is stickier, it's more likely to produce unwanted noises, and that you are less likely to get those unwanted noises if you use steel strings. On the other hand, rosins developed for steel strings are often harder than rosins intended especially for gut strings, because gut strings don't respond properly to a very hard rosin.

Harder rosin

Some experts – both violinists and rosin makers – say that harder rosins are more suitable for loud playing, where it is important that the strings respond immediately, and for music which requires a lot of pressure on the bow. But others, thinking of the unwanted noise problem again, recommend a harder rosin for quiet pieces.

Sticky

A very sticky rosin tends to produce less powder, so less gets onto your violin. What's more, you won't need to apply so much pressure on your bow. On the other hand, it's likely that you will have to clean your ribbon more often (or have it cleaned), which means it won't last as long.

Powder

Many experts believe the biggest difference between most rosins is the amount of powder they produce when you are applying them to the ribbon and just afterwards. Once you are playing, the difference between the various brands and series is often barely noticeable, if at all.

Expensive rosin

More expensive rosins are often finer in structure than cheap rosins. There is no point in buying expensive, fine rosin unless your bow is really worth it. The one thing most experts agree on is that the type of rosin you use makes little difference to a cheap bow. The cheapest rosins sell for £1/$3.

The average

Most rosins cost £3–6/$5–10, including varieties which contain gold or silver particles. Supposedly, these particles help produce greater clarity of sound, although not all violinists can tell the difference.

Trying out

If you buy a different bow, it may well be that you'll need a different rosin to do it justice. And it's the same story if you start using different strings. Unfortunately, choosing the right rosin remains a matter of trial and error. Try out a different type once in a while, just to see how it sounds and feels.

A rosin for each stick

Do remember though that experimenting is a slow process: the old rosin will still be audible for a good few hours after you've rubbed in a new rosin. There are violinists who use different rosins for different styles of music. That means they also need a different bow for each type of rosin.

The same name

Some manufacturers make it easy for you by giving their different rosins the same names as their strings. This can be a good starting point when choosing your rosin. Mind you, sometimes the very same rosin is sold in different tins and with different brand or series names, each with its own description.

Violin, viola, cello

One more example to demonstrate the range of opinions on this subject is that some manufacturers sell different rosins for violin, viola and cello, while others simply make a single rosin for all three instruments.

Allergies

If you are allergic to rosin, you can't really play the violin; there are no substitutes. If you are allergic to certain substances only used in certain rosins, try a different make. A rosin which produces less powder may also help.

8. ACCESSORIES

If you are to enjoy playing, you'll need a properly fitting chin rest and a comfortable shoulder rest. Other accessories for the violin are mutes, violin cases, and pickups or special violin microphones to amplify your violin.

The chin rest was not widely used until about a hundred and fifty years ago. Older violins can sometimes be recognized by a lighter coloured patch where the chins of former owners have worn away most of the varnish.

The shape of your chin
Whether you need a big chin rest or a small one, a deep one or a flat one depends on the shape of your chin. Some chin rests are a little higher than others, some are diamond-shaped.

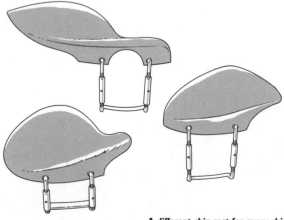

A different chin rest for every chin

Beside or above

You can choose a chin rest which sits right above the tailpiece, next to it, or somewhere in between. The closer the chin rest is to the tailpiece, the more your violin will be in line with your body when you play and vice versa. Some chin rests are adjustable, but most of them are set in one position.

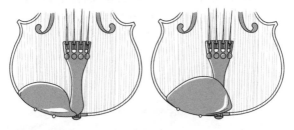

Chin rests in different places.

Names

Chin rests usually take the name of their designers, but some models are named after cities, or famous violin-makers – some of whom died long before the chin rest was invented!

Plastic, ebony, boxwood

Most models of chin rest are available in various materials. So you might find a particular model made from plastic for £4.50/$7 or from top quality ebony at five times the price. The more expensive models, selling for £30/$50 and above, are only available in the costlier woods, such as ebony, rosewood and boxwood.

Try a cloth

If you sweat rather heavily, it's a good idea to try a wooden chin rest first. On the other hand, if a wooden chin rest irritates your skin, you'll probably be better off with a plastic version. If you don't know whether it is the wood, the varnish or something else which is causing the problem, try playing with a cloth over the chin rest for a while – some violinists always play that way. You can also buy chin rests with a soft leather pad. Some people swear by them, others find that they get too hot for comfort.

Match your violin

Many violinists prefer a chin rest that matches the style and colour of the tailpiece, and of course goes with the rest of the violin. If you do too, it's worth knowing that you can buy ready-made sets with a chin rest, a tailpiece, an end-button and tuning pegs, all in the same colour and style.

Two feet

Most chin rests are attached to the violin body by two clamps or 'feet'. You tighten them by sticking a small key into a hole in the clamp and turning it (be careful not to damage the body), or by tightening little screws.

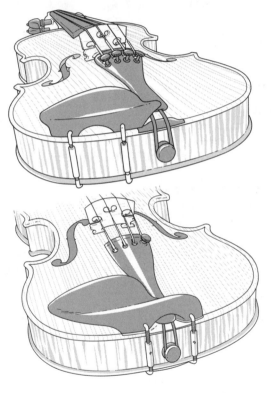

The clamps may be to the left of the end-button, or one on either side

Where?

Sometimes both clamps are attached to the left of the end-button, whilst other models have a clamp on either side of the end-button. Some violinists prefer the second type because the clamps are attached near the *bottom block*, a small wooden block inside the instrument that serves to reinforce the body at the end-button.

Turning the screw

A chin rest only touches the violin at the edges. To prevent damage, most chin rest clamps are covered with cork. If you tighten the clamps too far, you risk deforming the side of the body, but if your chin rest is too loose, it could slip off.

Small violins and violas

You can buy small chin rests for small violins and larger ones for violas. In both cases there is a narrower range of styles.

SHOULDER REST

The shoulder rest is an even more recent invention. It has only been widely used since the 1950s, and is still frowned upon by some violinists.

Higher up

Using a shoulder rest means that your violin sits a little higher, so you don't have to tilt your head as far to the left. On the other hand, you do need to lift your right arm higher, which some people dislike. A lower type of shoulder rest together with a higher chin rest can help you avoid such problems.

Pads and wooden rests

Some violinists still prefer the simplest shoulder rest of all: a small pad. Others use the traditional wooden shoulder rest, which is padded with soft material, covered with cloth and held in place by elastic bands.

More pads

For £4–10/$7–15 you can get a special pad which is attached to the body by a leather strap and an elastic band. If you have a long neck, choose a slightly fatter pad. You can also buy an inflatable pad and adjust its size and firmness to your own needs. Do be aware that the materials used for some pads can damage certain types of violin varnish.

Muffled?

Some violinists are against the use of pads, because they say they muffle the vibrations of the back of the instrument – not that most people can really hear the difference.

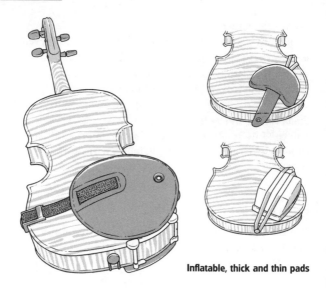

Inflatable, thick and thin pads

If you prefer using a pad but are concerned about muffling the tone, you can choose one attached to a 'bridge' so that it doesn't touch the back. This also helps prevent the varnish being rubbed away.

Adjustable

The most popular shoulder rests are made of a metal plate covered with soft rubber, which spans the back of the violin like a kind of bridge. They are attached by four clamps, which you can usually adjust to match the width of your instrument. Some types are also height-adjustable. Non-

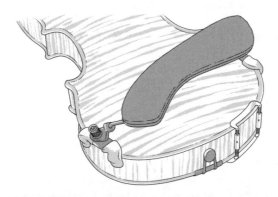

An adjustable metal shoulder rest with rubber covering

adjustable models often come in two or more heights. If you have a long neck, you'll probably need a higher shoulder rest.

Loose and fixed

The clamps of a shoulder rest are covered in a soft material so that they do not damage the varnish. Unlike chin rests, shoulder rests are supposed to be taken off the violin when it's not being played, so when trying out different models check how easy they are to attach and remove. Some models are collapsible so that they fit inside a case more easily.

Makes

Four well-known makes of shoulder rests are Johnson, Kun, Menuhin and Wolf. Some brands offer shoulder rests in bright colours alongside the many models in the more traditional black or brown.

MUTES

If you place a *mute* on the bridge of your instrument, the sound becomes softer, sweeter and warmer: mutes muffle some of the higher frequencies of the sound. If the composer wants you to use a mute, the score will show the instruction '*con sordino*' (*with mute*). From that point on, all the violins suddenly sound a lot more velvety. So-called practice mutes muffle the sound a lot more than ordinary mutes do. A wolf-note eliminator is yet another type of mute, with a very specific purpose.

Clothes peg

You may remember from chapter 5 that a heavy bridge can muffle the sound of your violin. A mute works in pretty much the same way. It makes the bridge heavier and the added material absorbs some of the vibrations. The larger or heavier the mute the stronger the effect, as you can see if you very carefully attach a wooden clothes peg to one side of the bridge, and then add another on the opposite side. You should notice that two pegs muffle the sound much more than one.

Rubber, metal, wood

Of course, the material itself also has an effect, and mutes may be made of rubber, metal or wood. Violinists often have several models. Mutes are very inexpensive, usually costing less than £3/$5.

Detachable and fixed

The most basic mute, a three-pronged model, looks like a short, fat comb, and is only attached to the instrument when its effect is required. Another type, *the fixed mute* or *slide-on mute*, stays attached to your strings. When it's not needed, you slide it down the strings towards the tailpiece. As well as rubber slide-on mutes you can find *wire mutes*, made of metal wire and a tube which muffles the strings.

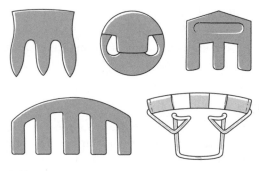

Detachable mutes

Quick

Sliding mutes are especially useful for pieces which ask you to change quickly between playing with and without a

A wire mute by the tailpiece...

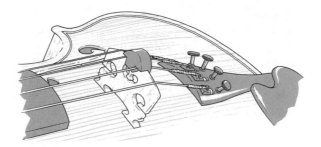

... and a rubber slide-on mute on the bridge

mute. However, some violinists don't use them, fearing that even when they are near the tailpiece they could muffle the sound (even though you're unlikely to hear the difference), or because they might vibrate along with the strings.

Small adjustments

You can also use a wire mute to make your sound just a tiny bit sweeter. To do so, slide it to a position between the bridge and the tailpiece. The closer you get to the bridge, the stronger the muffling effect. You can also set a wire mute diagonally, so that you muffle the high strings more than the low ones or the other way around.

Practice mute

If you want to practice without bothering everyone around you, you can buy a big, soft, practice mute. The drawback of using a practice mute is that it muffles the sound so much that you won't be able to hear yourself properly: it's not a good solution if you're working on your tone or bowing technique.

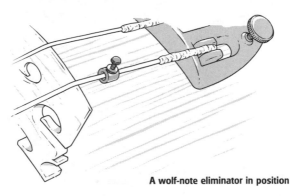

A wolf-note eliminator in position

Wolf note

Occasionally, a violin will produce a *wolf note*, a note that seems to 'stutter'. You can usually put an end to this problem with a *wolf-note eliminator*. This is nothing more than a very short metal cylinder attached to the stuttering string between bridge and tailpiece. It takes a little trial and error to find the most effective position.

VIOLIN CASES

Violins are not generally sold complete with case, except for some cheaper models. It is an essential, and you will need to buy one.

Oblong or violin-shaped

Cases are available in a variety of styles. As well as the rectangular type, there are cases whose shape matches the shape of the instrument. A rectangular case usually has an extra large compartment to store your shoulder rest and a set of spare strings, a mute, rosin and the like.

The case and the lining

The case itself usually has a hard shell, made of wood or synthetic material, covered with plastic, cloth or leather. Cases often use thermoplastic, an insulating synthetic which

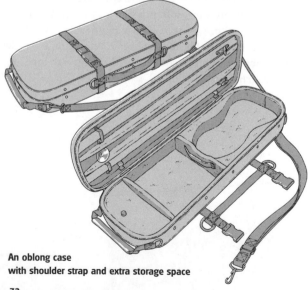

**An oblong case
with shoulder strap and extra storage space**

shields the instrument from temperature and humidity changes.

Waterproof
A case or bag must be waterproof, so check that it closes properly. Cases with a cloth lining sometimes have a separate flap to protect the opening. Loose covers are also available, often with a separate pocket for sheet music.

Locks
Most cases are lockable. This is mainly to ensure that the catches cannot open accidentally, for instance if you drop your case. If you get into the habit of always locking the catches, you can be sure that they will always be fastened properly. The locks won't stop thieves: if someone has their eye on your violin, they'll be happy to have a case to go with it.

Locks and hinges
Always check locks, hinges, handles and carrying straps carefully, because they are the places where cases are most likely to break.

Protection
A good case will absorb a shock if it falls. It should also be sturdy enough to resist being crushed if something heavy falls on it. A very cheap case may not offer enough protection.

Around six pounds
The lightest cases of all only weigh a couple of pounds, but you can buy cases that weigh three times as much. Very light models are usually less shockproof than heavier ones. A violin itself weighs about a pound.

Inside
Many cases have a strip of velcro to hold the neck in place. This will also stop your violin from falling out if you accidentally open the case the wrong way up. All cases have a soft interior to absorb shocks, and usually the more expensive the case, the thicker the padding. Many cases are deeper near the neck of the violin, so that this vulnerable part does not touch the bottom of the case.

Cloth

If you cover your violin with a cloth the instrument cannot be damaged by your bow, which fits into the inside of the lid. You sometimes get a cloth when you buy a case, or you can buy one separately. Instead of using a cloth, some people put the violin in a bag, often made of silk.

Containers and cylinders

The inside of the lid usually has space to hold two bows. A tip: put the bows in with their ribbons facing away from one another. If you use wound gut strings, which should not be rolled up, you keep your spare strings in a special string cylinder.

Rucksack

Some cases have rucksack straps already attached, but others can be fitted with them separately.

Smaller and bigger

Small cases are usually no cheaper than full-size ones, but viola cases, being slightly bigger, are more expensive. Because violas vary in size, viola cases come in different sizes too. The more expensive models are often adjustable. For people who use more than one instrument, there are cases designed to hold two or even four violins or violas.

Prices

You can expect to pay at least £75/$100 for a case that can really take a knock, but you can get cheaper ones too. A case covered with leather will easily cost ten times as much.

Hygrometer

Violins are particularly sensitive to very dry air. Some of the more expensive cases available have their own hygrometer, a device that shows how much moisture there is in the air. You can read more about hygrometers on page 95.

AMPLIFIED VIOLINS

If you play your violin in a band, you're likely to find that it isn't loud enough. You can of course solve the problem with an ordinary microphone, but there are better solutions.

Microphones

Playing the violin with an ordinary microphone of the type singers use is tricky because if you move away or get closer the volume will vary. What's more, there's a good chance you'll get *feedback*. That's the horrible high-pitched squeal you hear if someone holds a microphone too close to a loudspeaker.

Pickups

Instead of a microphone, you can use one or two *pickups*. These are small, thin 'plates' made of a special material which pick up the vibrations of your strings and convert them into electrical signals. Most violin pickups are made to fit into the openings in the side of the bridge. Because your bridge will usually need some filing to get a good fit, and because the precise positioning is very important to the sound, it's best to let an expert install them for you. The jack for the amplifier lead (US cable) is usually attached to the side of the violin with a clamp.

Pickup

Less warm

If you use a pickup, you can turn up the amplifier quite a way before you get feedback, but the sound is usually a little harsher than when you play acoustically.

Microphones

Instead of using a pickup, you could use a special miniature microphone clipped onto the instrument. This type of microphone gives you more of the 'real' sound of your violin, although the risk of feedback does increase. In other words, you can't play as loudly with one of these microphones as you can with a pickup.

Microphone

Cotton wool

A trick to prevent feedback, if you do need to play really loudly, is to fill your violin with bits of cotton wool. You can easily get them out again with a crochet needle.

Prices and brands

The very cheapest pickups cost less than £30/$50. Professional standard pickups cost two or three times as much. Well-known makes include Barcus Berry, Fishman, Seymour Duncan and Shadow. Violin microphones cost more. The Dutch manufacturer SD Systems makes a device which combines a microphone with a single pickup, allowing you to choose the proportion of each you use. Some violinists use a pickup on their violin together with a ordinary microphone on a stand.

Electric violin and tuners

Of course, you can also choose an electric violin. You can read more about them in chapter 12, *The Family*. If you are using a microphone, you'll probably be amplified by the band's or the venue's PA system. If you decide to buy your own amplifier, you're best off with the type of amplifier used by acoustic guitarists.

9. TUNING

A violin needs to be tuned before you can play it. When you start out your teacher will tune it for you, but sooner or later you'll have to learn to do it yourself. Is it difficult? No. But you'll only learn properly by doing it often. This chapter tells you how to go about it.

A violin won't easily go out of tune if it's in good condition. Even so, you always need to check the tuning before you start playing. If you have them, fine tuners are usually all you need to adjust the tuning.

Big and awkward

If you haven't been playing for very long, you probably use steel or synthetic strings. These kinds of strings are very awkward to tune with the wooden tuning pegs: you only have to turn them a little bit too far and before you know it the string is too slack or too tight. If you're not careful, you could even tighten it so much that it breaks.

Tuning as you bow

Plucking or bowing?

You can sound the string you are tuning by plucking, as you would with a guitar. For beginners that's easier, but you'll hear what you're doing better if you bow the strings. Before you can do either, you'll have to learn how to hold your violin under your chin whilst you bow or pluck with your right hand and operate the fine tuners or pegs with your left.

The notes

The strings of violin and viola are tuned to the following notes:

	Violin	Viola
String 1	E	A (thinnest, highest sounding string)
String 2	A	D
String 3	D	G
String 4	G	C (thickest, lowest sounding string)

The A

Most instruments are tuned to the A that sounds the same pitch as the A-string of a well-tuned violin or viola. If a string sounds at this pitch, it is vibrating at 440 times per second. Technically, the note is called A440 (A = 440 hertz).

Piano or tuning fork

The A-string is the first string to tune. You can match this string to the same A on the piano: it's the A slightly to the right of the centre of the keyboard, and is called a1 (see page 12–13). If you don't have a piano you can buy a tuning fork. This is a thick, two-pronged metal fork which you first tap on your knee and then press against your ear by the stem. The note you hear is the A you need. A tuning fork will only cost you £3/$5. Some orchestras tune to an A which is a tiny bit higher. You can buy different tuning forks for these tunings too, such as A442.

Tuning fork

Too high, too low?

The first string you tune is always the A. Listen to the A of the tuning fork or piano and turn the fine tuner until the string sounds at the same pitch. When you are learning to tune your violin it can be difficult to hear whether a string is too high or too low. If so, first turn the fine tuner all the way down. Then you can be almost certain the string is tuned too low. From there, slowly go back up.

Singing

You can also sing along. First sing the note of the tuning fork or piano, and then the note made by the string. If you now find yourself singing higher, you'll know whether you need to tune the string higher or lower. A tip: if you have a piano handy, play an A and keep the right pedal pressed down so that the note will keep sounding for a long time, making it easier to compare.

In the middle

If you start with the fine tuner in the 'middle setting', you can usually tune the A-string up or down by a whole tone or even more. In most cases, this is enough.

The E

Once the A is in tune, go on to the E-string. You can find this E on a piano too (e2), but you can also do it without one. Try singing the first two words of *Twinkle, Twinkle, Little Star*. The second *Twinkle* sounds a perfect fifth higher than the first, and that's exactly the interval you need. Play the A-string and sing the first *Twinkle* at that pitch. Then tune the E-string to the note you make when you sing the second *Twinkle*. When you've done that, it will be at the right pitch.

Another fifth

Next, tune the D-string. The D is a fifth lower than the A. There's another song you can use to find the D: *What Shall We Do With The Drunken Sailor*. Sing the first words as you play the A-string, and then tune the D-string to the note you sing for the syllable *-ken*.

G, D and C

You then tune the G from the D-string in the same way. On a viola you begin with the A-string, naturally, and from there go to the D, the G and finally the C. Once you have tuned all four strings, check them again. Usually you'll have to adjust the tuning here or there, if only because it's not easy to sing exactly in tune. But still, these songs will point you in the right direction.

Better still

A good way to hear whether you need to adjust your tuning is to bow two adjacent strings. On a properly tuned violin, these 'string pairs' produce a pleasant, full sound. If a pair produces a slightly 'wavy' sound, they're not quite in tune, so carefully adjust the tuning. The slower the waves get, the closer you are. As soon as the waves disappear, you're in tune.

Don't press

If you are adjusting your fine tuners as you bow, there's a good chance you'll press them down slightly without meaning to. As soon as you let go, the pitch will go down and you'll have to start again. So the way to do it is to first adjust, then let go and listen, then adjust again, and so on.

Bowing

Also, when you are concentrating on tuning, your bowing may change, influencing the exact pitch you produce. Then, when you start playing normally again, you'll hear that you need to adjust the tuning after all. In other words, when you are tuning, make sure you bow the same way as you always do. Of course, that's easier said than done.

With a piano

You can of course tune all your strings with a piano, but you'll learn to tune better if you tune from the A-string. After all, that's how you'll have to do it if you play in an orchestra.

Pitch pipe

Pitch pipes are popular tuning aids. There are two types, those with one note (the A) and those with four (one for each string). Pitch pipes are cheap, but they tend to go out of tune quickly. Besides, it's easier to compare your A-string with a tuning fork.

Tuner

A *chromatic tuner* is much more advanced. It's an electronic device which tells you exactly which note is being played, and whether the note is too low, too high or exactly right. Prices start at around £15/$25. Chromatic tuners are especially popular with guitarists, but violinists often say it's better to learn to tune by ear, because you depend on your ear to tell you whether you are playing out of tune – which is much less of a problem for guitarists.

A little higher

Strings stretch as they get older, which can mean you won't be able to tighten them enough with the fine tuners. If this happens you'll have to tune them a little higher with the pegs. Before you do, first loosen the string with the fine tuner as far as it will go. Also check the underside of the tailpiece now and then, to make sure your fine tuners will not damage the belly of your instrument when tightening the strings.

Tuning with pegs

When you tune with your pegs, it's easiest if you 'tune upwards': if a string sounds too high, first turn the peg until the string sounds too low and then go back up from there. Apart from that, tuning with pegs is really the same as tuning with fine tuners – though it may take some time to learn how to adjust them.

Scordatura

Very occasionally, violins are tuned differently. For example, the pitch of the lowest string might be reduced by a whole tone or a semitone. Such alternative tunings are known as *scordatura*. They are more common in folk styles.

10. VIOLIN MAINTENANCE

Real repairs and setting-up are best left to an expert. But there is plenty you can do yourself to keep your instrument in the best possible condition: cleaning, replacing strings, straightening the bridge, finding buzzes, and much more.

The rosin from your bow lands on your violin as powder. Wipe it off with a soft, lint-free cloth each time you finish playing. A cotton cloth will be fine: an old plain T-shirt for instance, or a dishcloth. With older instruments especially, watch out for splinters around the edges. And don't forget to clean the stick of the bow too.

Fingerboard and strings

It's best to use a different cloth for the neck, strings and fingerboard, where you touch them with your fingers. Wipe the strings with the cloth and then pull it between the fingerboard and the strings. Again, a cotton cloth is good for the job, but some violinists prefer to use silk. Once you've cleaned your violin, put it back in its case.

Prevention

Strings will stay playable longer if you wash your hands before you touch them, and your violin will be easier to keep clean if you only hold it by the neck and in the area of the chin rest.

Cleaners

Every violin needs extra attention once in a while, even if you are careful with it. The belly can get sticky and dull, especially between the f-holes where most of the rosin ends up. You can remove the build-up of rosin with a special violin cleaner. Some cleaners polish as well as clean, smoothing away fine scratches. You can also buy special violin cleaning cloths, impregnated with polish which is released when you use them. On most violins, you can remove surface dust and dirt with a slightly damp cloth. Do make sure you don't touch the strings.

The best?
Which is the best cleaner for your violin depends partly on the varnish used. So always ask what you can and cannot use on an instrument when you buy or rent it.

Never
Whatever you do, never use ordinary household cleaners. Also, when you are cleaning your violin avoid touching it anywhere where it is damaged, as this will make it harder to repair.

The fingerboard
You can occasionally give the fingerboard an extra clean by dabbing it with a soft cloth moistened with a little methylated spirits. To make absolutely sure that none of the meths gets onto the varnish of the body, keep the bottle well out of the way and do not allow the cloth to drag over the body. For safety's sake you can lay another dry cloth over the body to protect it.

The strings
It is a good idea to remove the rosin residue from your strings from time to time. Take a cloth and push it along the strings a few times from the top of the fingerboard to the bridge. Don't push too hard, and damp the strings with one hand, because they can really screech when you do this. A cloth with meths will work for strings too, and you can even buy special string cleaners. *String oil* is meant for non-wound gut strings only, and stops them drying out.

Inside
Over the course of the years, dust and dirt will inevitably find its way inside your violin. To get it out, pour in half a

handful of dry, uncooked rice and carefully shake it backwards and forwards through the body a few times. Then tip the violin upside down and carefully shake it to let the rice run out, cleaning the underside of the belly as you do so. Most of the dust will come out with the rice.

Check
You should regularly inspect your violin for splinters or other minor damage. Also check whether the chin rest is still secure, and that the padding on the clamps of your shoulder rest is not torn.

Expert
There are times when you'll need to take your violin to an expert. When it needs more extensive cleaning, if there are stains which won't go away or you can't get the neck properly clean, or if the varnish is becoming very dull (on the body, under the strings, or where you touch the body with your left hand).

Many violinists have their instruments checked once a year, even if there is nothing wrong with them, just to be on the safe side.

Plastic
If your sweat is especially acidic, it can damage the varnish and even the wood of the ribs by the shoulder of the violin where your left hand touches it. The solution? Have a strip of self-adhesive plastic stuck to the shoulder. Admittedly, some people are appalled by the very idea while others see it as simply being practical.

TUNING PEGS AND FINE TUNERS
Fine tuners do not require much maintenance, if any. If one does get a little stiff, smear on a tiny bit of acid-free vaseline. Wooden tuning pegs, on the other hand, can be troublesome.

Peg compound
The tuning pegs need to be able to turn smoothly, without slipping back. If they get stuck or they slip, try using a little *peg compound*, *peg paste* or *peg dope*. A stop-gap solution for slipping pegs is to rub them with a piece of chalk.

Loose

If a peg or the hole is badly worn, it may get really loose. Having a new set of fatter pegs made to measure costs around £40–60/$50–75. That's unless you choose really expensive ones: you can buy pegs with golden rings or other expensive decorations at £20/$25 each, if not more. If the hole is too big even for a fatter peg, you can have it filled up (reshaped), but that can easily cost £30/$50.

BOW

Maintaining your bow basically comes down to applying rosin to it, and very occasionally you should clean the ribbon thoroughly, or have it cleaned. Rehairing is, of course, a job for a craftsperson.

Rosin

Applying rosin is only necessary when the ribbon gets too smooth. That shouldn't happen more often than once every week, even if you play a lot. Move the ribbon over the rosin rather than the other way around, applying the rosin along the full length of the ribbon, from the head to the frog. If you keep your thumb on the ferrule, you can stop it from damaging the rosin.

Stray rosin

Wipe the ribbon with a cloth when you have finished, or drag one of your nails across the bowhairs close to the frog. This makes sure that the excess rosin doesn't land on your violin. You can shake out your bow instead, but it's best not to; you can still damage your bow even if you don't hit anything.

Cleaning

The ribbon often gets a bit grimy near the frog. You can clean it with a cloth dipped in lukewarm water and possibly a little washing-up liquid. The ends of the ribbon are

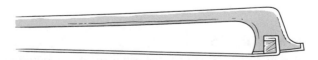

The ribbon is held in place by small wooden wedges

held in place by small wooden wedges: be sure not to get them wet.

Too smooth

If you find you need to put fresh rosin on more and more frequently, that's probably due to a build-up of rosin residue which makes the hair smooth. You can clean it off yourself with a cloth and a 70% alcohol cleaner, but it's safer to have it done by an expert, since alcohol can easily damage the stick, and you may end up making the bowhairs stick together even more than before. A craftsperson can decide whether cleaning will help, or whether the ribbon needs replacing.

Broken hairs

If a hair breaks, remove the loose ends by 'tearing' them on the sharp edge of the ferrule or the face, rather than simply pulling them out. Another solution is to cut them carefully with scissors, as close as possible to the ferrule or face.

Too slack

If you can't get the bow to the correct tension, you may have an overstretched ribbon, or your bow could be slowly straightening out. An expert may be able to restore its original curve. If the hair is overstretched, you'll never get the bow back to proper tension: the usual solution is a new ribbon, although the ribbon can sometimes be shortened. The same is true if too many of the hairs have broken. A rehair usually costs between £30–40/$40–50. If you only play for a few hours a week, your ribbon will last for years.

Sliding smoothly

The frog and the adjuster are quite easy to loosen if they are no longer sliding and turning smoothly. If you turn the screw completely loose, you can take the frog from the bow stick. Simply cleaning it often helps. If not, it's best to have the bow looked at. You should do the same if the lapping or winding are worn out, or if the frog seems to be loose.

NEW STRINGS

If your strings break or if the windings come loose, you need to replace them. The same is true if they are too old:

old strings get harder to tune and sound dull. The better your violin is, the better your playing and the better your ear, the sooner you'll notice when one or more strings need to be replaced.

How long
Its impossible to say exactly how long a set of strings will last. If you have synthetic strings and you play for a few hours a week, you might try fitting new strings after six months or so. If you hear the difference straightaway, try replacing the new set after just four months. If you can't hear any difference after six months, wait a little longer before replacing your strings next time. Your strings will always last longer if you keep your strings and your hands clean, and if your sweat isn't too acidic.

Longer
Steel strings usually last a bit longer than synthetic strings, and gut strings wear out the quickest. When should you replace your strings? When plucking them only produces a short, dull tone it's a sign that they are wearing out. If they become discoloured, you're also better off replacing them. But do note that silver-wound strings may still be fine long after they have begun to discolour.

Aluminium
Some windings, aluminium ones for example, are easily damaged by certain types of sweat. If you see this happening, try using a set of strings with a different type of winding, such as chrome-steel.

A new set
If one of your wound strings breaks, the new string you fit may sound a lot brighter than the older ones. If it does, the only solution is to replace the other wound strings too. Used strings can still be used as emergency spares.

A new E
You can usually fit a new plain E without replacing the other strings. Some violinists think their instrument sounds better if they use cheap E strings and replace them frequently rather than stick with an expensive E-string for longer.

Not more than two

Before replacing your strings, lay your violin on a folded towel on a flat surface, or on your lap. An important tip: don't loosen more than two strings at a time, so that the other strings hold the bridge and soundpost in place. If the soundpost does fall over despite your precautions, loosen all the strings and have it set in position by an expert before you start playing again.

The middle string

The two outer strings pass below the middle ones in the pegbox, which makes them harder to reach. So first loosen one of the two middle strings, and then the string which passes below it. First replace the outer string, and then the middle one.

Loosening

To loosen a string, turn the tuning peg towards you and pull it outwards slightly. Then pull gently on the string, so the peg will start turning until the string comes loose. Guide the string between your thumb and index finger near the pegbox, so that it can't suddenly come loose and damage your eyes, the varnish or anything else.

Cut

You can also turn the peg until the string is slack and then cut it by the pegbox. It is easier and safer to remove the short end than the whole string. You can use a small pair of pliers to work the last bit free from the peg.

Fitting strings

You can fit new strings in various ways. This is one simple way.
- Turn the peg so that the hole points diagonally upwards, facing the fingerboard.
- Attach the string to the tailpiece.
- Poke the string through the peg and start winding it; make sure the hole moves in the direction of the scroll.
- Hold the string with your other hand so that it can't go slack and slip out of the hole or come loose from the tailpiece.
- Keep on tightening the string, making sure that the windings run outwards, towards the fatter end of the peg.

Keep the string tight and guide it through the groove in the nut with your index finger.
- Tune it so that it is at roughly the right tension, comparing it to the strings that are still in place.

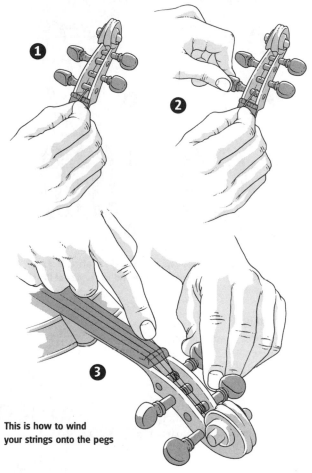

This is how to wind your strings onto the pegs

Kink

You may find that a string keeps on coming loose from the peg as you try to tighten it. If so, take a small pair of pliers and make a kink about half an inch (1–1.5cm) long at the very end of the string. Poke that piece through the hole. The string will hook itself in place as you begin to turn.

Firmly fixed

There's another way you can be sure your strings will stay

firmly fixed. Make a kink in the same way as before, and lay the kinked piece flat against the peg. Then let the string run over it a couple of times as you turn the peg. Please note: do not twist the plain (non-wound) part of a wound string around itself.

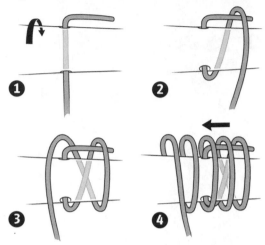

This way, the strings will always stay properly in place. Make a kink in the string, lay it against the peg and let the rest of the string wind around it.

Long strings

If a string is very long, you can first let it wind inwards for a few turns, before guiding it back the other way. The last few turns must be wound directly onto the wood, and not on top of another part of the string.

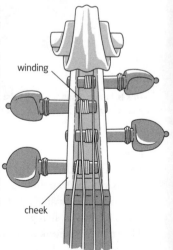

Space

Strings can break if they are jammed against the cheeks of the pegbox. So always make sure they have some space.

String sleeves

If you use string sleeves (see page 52), slide them into place

Leave space between windings and cheeks.

when the strings are nearly tuned. A sleeve does the most good on the E-string. Instead of a sleeve, many violinists lay a tiny piece of vellum (parchment) under the string instead.

Protection
If you do want to use fine tuners for your gut strings, then buy a type which is specially made for these strings. Other types will cut through the loop of the string in no time.

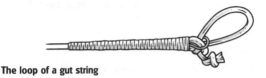

The loop of a gut string

The first time
When you are replacing a string for the first time, you'll probably find you don't have enough hands. You need one to tighten, another to make sure the string doesn't come loose from the tailpiece and another to guide it through the right grooves in the bridge and nut, so it's handy to have someone else around to help.

Grooves
Check the pegs when replacing strings. Grooves in the pegs can make your strings break. If the pegs won't grip the strings whatever you do, there's a chance that the holes are worn out.

Other causes
Other things that can easily damage strings are sharp edges on the bridge, the nut, or around the string-holes in the pegs. The grooves in the nut must be smooth and nicely rounded to prevent the strings from kinking. Check your violin carefully if a string keeps breaking at the same point. If a string doesn't run smoothly across the nut or the bridge, twist the point of a soft pencil through the groove a few times. If that doesn't do the trick, you'll need expert help.

Perfect fifths
On a properly tuned violin, there is always a perfect fifth between one string and the next (see pages 11 and 79). You

can check this by laying a pencil across two strings and pressing down so that they both touch the fingerboard. In both high and low positions, the difference in pitch between the two strings should always be a perfect fifth. If you have old strings, this may not be so, perhaps because one string is more stretched than the other. If so, the first will sound too low. On the other hand, a new string might sound 'too high' if you fit it between two older ones. Old strings are not the only possible cause if you don't hear perfect fifths; the bridge may be the problem instead.

THE BRIDGE

The bridge is held in place by the strings. At the same time, the strings pull it forwards and push it down, bending it slightly. Altogether, the bridge has to withstand a pressure of around sixty pounds. In other words, it has a tough time, and you need to keep an eye on it.

Leaning

Now and then, you should check that the bridge hasn't started leaning forwards, towards the fingerboard. You can straighten it yourself, carefully, but if you haven't been playing very long it's definitely better to get someone to do it for you. Make sure one foot of the bridge is not further forward than the other. If it is, you won't hear perfect fifths when you do the test on the previous page.

New bridge

If the pressure of the strings has forced the bridge to bend, you need a new one. The bridge also needs replacing if the grooves are too deep: no more than a third of the diameter of each string should be inside the groove. If you switch to different strings you may find that the action needs to be adjusted, which in turn means you'll need a new or

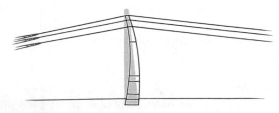

Bridge bending towards the fingerboard

modified bridge. You might choose to have your bridge replaced if the belly is too flat (so that you keep touching two strings instead of one), or is too curved (making it difficult to play two or three strings at once if you want to).

Cutting a bridge

Every bridge must be made to measure so that it has the right height and curve, and so that the feet fit the belly perfectly. Having a bridge cut usually costs £30–50/$50–75. A new bridge should last for years.

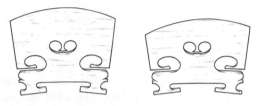

A blank bridge and one made to measure

OTHER POINTS

A violin is a fragile and sensitive instrument, and it only gives its best if everything is in place, nothing is loose and producing a buzz, and if nothing is worn out.

The soundpost and the tailgut

If you have bought a new violin, it's a good idea to have it checked after six months. Here are a couple of examples of things an expert might spot: the soundpost may have become slightly too short as a result of the wood not having settled completely when you bought the instrument, or the tailgut may have stretched. If so, the distance between tailpiece and bridge will now be too short, giving a muffled sound. The correct distance is somewhere between about 2.2 and 2.4 inches (5.5 – 6cm) on a violin, and an extra 0.4 inches (1cm) on a viola.

The fingerboard

However hard your fingerboard is, the strings will make grooves in it eventually. Also, your fingers will make very shallow pits in it over the course of time, especially if you sweat a lot. Of course, if you have a good fingerboard this is a very slow process. As an example, professional violinists, who play for many hours every day, often have their fingerboards reworked once a year or every two years. If your fingerboard has been reworked too often, you can have a new one fitted to your violin for around £100–200/ $150–250.

Loose pieces

If a piece of your violin breaks off, for instance along the edge, make sure that no moisture reaches that spot, and don't clean it. Take the instrument to a violin maker as soon as possible, and take the broken-off piece with you if you still have it. It's also best to see an expert if you find loose glue seams or cracks. Tempted to glue them yourself? Don't.

Buzzes

A violin can start buzzing in all sorts of places. For example:
- The nut or the saddle may have come loose without you noticing.
- The winding of a string may be damaged.
- If the bridge or the nut are too low it will affect the action, letting the strings vibrate against the fingerboard.
- Another place to look if you are trying to find a buzz is at the ends of the strings: they may vibrate if they are touching the pegbox or tailpiece.
- The tailpiece itself should not be touching the belly or the chin rest at any point.

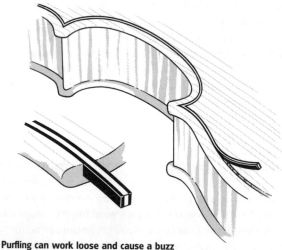

Purfling can work loose and cause a buzz

- Is the chin rest securely fastened?
- Are the sleeves around the strings in the right place?
- A wire mute or loose purfling can also cause unwanted noises, and so can an inlaid eye or a decorative button on a tuning peg.
- There are other possible causes.

DRY AIR

Wooden instruments are especially sensitive to dry air. And they don't like rapid changes from dry to moist or hot to cold.

Freezing

Dry air is especially likely to be a problem if it is freezing outside and the central heating is on full blast. If it gets too dry, the wood of your instrument will shrink too much. The result? If you're lucky, all that will happen is that the tuning pegs will suddenly come loose. If you're unlucky, the belly, the back or any other part may crack.

Hygrometer

The best level of humidity, both for violins and for people, is around fifty or sixty percent. You can keep an eye on the humidity if you have a hygrometer in the room, and there are violin cases that have one built-in. If this measuring device shows that the air is getting too dry, it's time to do something about it.

Humidifiers

There are all kinds of small humidifiers that can be used inside the case, ranging from a very basic rubber tube with holes in it and a small sponge inside to more complicated devices, some with a simple hygrometer built in. Prices are around £8/$11. Putting a few slices of potato inside your case is a good stop-gap solution.

The room

Of course, you can also increase the air humidity in the room where the violin is kept and played. Tubs of water attached to the radiator may not be enough if it's freezing hard outside. For £35/$50 you can buy a hot water humidifier, which vaporizes water by boiling it off very gently.

There are quieter devices available, but they cost more. If you need a very cheap and effective short-term solution, then hang a few wet towels over the radiators.

Getting used to it
Have you just come out of the rain into a dry room or into a warm house from the cold? Or the other way around? Leave your violin in its case for a while to let it acclimatize gradually.

Never!
And of course you should never leave your violin in direct sunlight, close to a heater or anywhere else where it could get too hot, too cold, too wet or too dry – not even if it's in its case.

ON THE ROAD
A few tips for when you travel with your violin:
- Make sure you have a **good case**, and check now and again to make sure that the handles and carrying straps are properly secured (see page 72).
- In the car, your violin is **safest** between the back seat and the front seats. The temperature is likely to be more stable there than in the boot (US trunk), and the chance of damage if you have an accident is smaller too. The worst place is under the dashboard, when the sun is shining, in full view of anyone who might fancy a violin.
- And when you're in the train, tram, tube (subway) or bus, keep your violin **on your lap**. That's the safest place, and you're less likely to forget it.
- If you still leave your violin behind somewhere, you're more likely to get it back if **your name**, address and phone number are written down somewhere inside your violin case.
- A **separate insurance** policy for your violin can't do any harm. Musical instruments are 'valuables', so ordinary household insurance will by no means cover all damage – whether it occurs at home or while travelling, on stage or in the rehearsal room. You can also take out special musical instrument insurance policies (see page 120).
- At the back of this book there is space to note down **the most important details** about your violin. Write them

down now, before somebody walks off with it. If you have an expensive instrument and you want it insured, you will need to have it appraised first. The appraisal report will state what the violin is worth and will also note all kinds of identifying features.

11. BACK IN TIME

You could write shelves and shelves of books on the violin and its centuries-old history, and there are plenty of writers who have done just that. That's why the history chapter in this book has been kept nice and short.

People have written so much about the history of the violin because it's a fascinating story and a very long one, and also because there is disagreement about many parts of the story. A few things are known for sure, though.

Bow and arrow

Thousands of years ago, when humans still hunted for their food with bows and arrows, the hunters noticed that you hear a note when you shoot an arrow: the vibration of the bowstring.

The eighth century

The fact that you can also make a string vibrate by bowing it was only discovered much later. Exactly when is not certain, but it is known that bowed string instruments were being played in ancient Persia and some other places, by the eighth century BCE. They are first recorded in Europe some time in the ninth century CE.

Fiddle

The name fiddle is sometimes used to describe all the string instruments from the Middle Ages, and there were quite a few. One of the best-known descendants of these fiddles is the *lyre*, an instrument that was built in various sizes. Lyres often had ten or more strings, plus a pair of

bourdon or drone strings, also called sympathetic strings. These strings are not bowed, but vibrate quietly in the background. The lyre is often seen as the predecessor of the violin.

Viola da gamba

The first viola da gamba were built around the fifteenth century. These instruments are played with the neck in an upright position, the smaller sizes resting on the knee of the musician, the larger ones held between the legs: gamba is Italian for leg. Some of the very large versions would simply rest on the ground like a double bass.

On your arm

The violins we know today are descended from a different family, that of the viola da braccio. Braccio is Italian for arm, and the

Viola da gamba, an instrument with six strings

German Bratsche (for viola) is derived from this word. Originally, these instruments really were played resting on the arm. Only later were they held under the chin.

The difference

The gambas were not just held in a different way to the braccios, they also look different. For instance, they have 'drooping' shoulders and more strings, and they're tuned differently. They also have frets, just like a guitar: thin strips set across the fingerboard which make it easier to play in tune: it is the position of the fret that produces the right pitch, not the exact position of the finger. On a gamba, the frets are made of gut strings fitted around the neck.

Amateurs and professional

There is another difference. Gambas, with a more delicate, softer sound, were mainly played by rich amateur musicians. Braccios, by contrast, were especially popular with folk musicians, who often earned their living by playing. With a violin on your arm you can dance and walk around as you play, and a violin produces more volume, always useful at parties. Around two hundred years ago, the gambas gradually disappeared from the scene, and today they are rarely played.

The cello and the bass
The cello is actually a member of the braccio family, but because it is so big, you rest it on the floor between your legs as you would a gamba. The double bass is related to both the braccios and the gambas. You can read more about both instruments in the next chapter.

Amati and Stradivarius
The first violins were built in the first half of the sixteenth century. One of those early violins, built by Andrea Amati, has even survived. Antonio Stradivari, who is often called Stradivarius, made the violin a little flatter around 1700, resulting in a stronger sound. This change was not immediately popular, because people were used to the softer sound of violins with a higher arching. But in the century that followed, the demand for louder violins grew, especially since music was being performed in ever larger halls.

From straight to curved
In the same period, the bow changed too. Curving the stick, which was originally straight, meant that the musician could play with more force.

Strings
The very first violins had unwound gut strings. As early as the seventeenth century, it was discovered that the strings themselves could be made thinner if they were wound, and that these thin, wound strings were easier to play. The steel E-string became popular about a hundred years ago, and the other steel strings followed about twenty years later. Synthetic strings are only fifty years old.

12. THE FAMILY

The cello and the double bass are the two best-known relatives of the violin. But of course there are many more related instruments old and new, from the rabab to the kemenche and from the Hardanger fiddle to the electric violin.

First the cello, which is not very different from the violin or the viola. The main difference is that it's quite a lot bigger. The cello is tuned in the same way as a viola, only an octave lower (eight white keys on the piano). Often the instrument is still called by its old, official name: *violoncello.* Around 1700, Stradivarius built a cello which is still used as the standard model.

Double bass

The double bass looks like an even bigger violin, but actually there are quite a few differences. It is not so much a big brother as a distant cousin. Unlike a violin, the bass usually has sloping shoulders and the back is often flat. The tuning is different too: E, A, D, G, from low to high (the same as a bass guitar). The double bass is often used outside classical music, particularly in jazz, when it is usually plucked instead of bowed.

Bourdon strings

Most of the other relatives are rare. The old *viola d'amore*, for instance: this is a kind of gamba with sympathetic strings (see page 99) which is played like a violin. The Norwegian *hardingfele* (Hardanger fiddle) is a smaller type of violin with four sympathetic strings.

Rabab

There are many other bowed instruments with sympathetic strings. The Afghan *rabab* shown in the drawing has twelve, although that's only one kind: there are rababs that have just two bowed strings, and no bourdon strings at all. Just like fiddle, *rebec* and *kemenche*, rabab is a name used for a whole series of different bowed instruments.

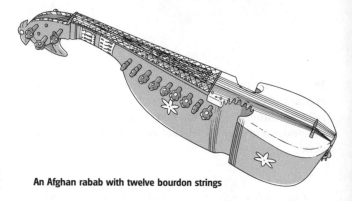

An Afghan rabab with twelve bourdon strings

Pear-shaped or elongated

A kemenche is a small, pear-shaped bowed instrument with three strings used in Turkish classical music. But it can also be an elongated three-stringed instrument used to play folk music in the Black Sea area and in Greece. The spelling varies as much as the shape, from *kemânje* to *kamaché*. Most of these instruments are played on the knee, with the neck held upright. You may even see musicians who play an ordinary violin in the same way. And rebecs? The name is used for a host of instruments, with two, three or more strings, with round or octagonal bodies and with or without frets

With a fingernail

With some of these instruments, the different notes are made not by stopping the strings on the fingerboard, but by touching them very lightly with a fingernail. The bow stick is often straight, and you tension the hairs not with a frog but simply by putting your fingers or thumb between the stick and the ribbon.

Fiddles

Fiddles are still built today, in different sizes and tunings.

Like gambas they have frets. The name fiddle is also still used as a kind of general term for string instruments, from one-stringed Indian to tubular North American Indian models. Of course, the word *fiddle* also simply means violin.

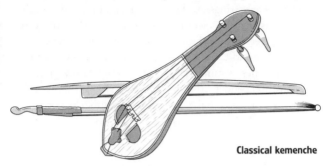

Classical kemenche

Very different
A violin is not the easiest instrument to hold, and some violinists develop problems with their neck, arms or fingers. All kinds of variations have been tried, especially with violas, to solve this problem. An example is the Pelegrina by the American violist and violin maker David Rivinus.

The Pelegrina

ELECTRIC VIOLINS
Electric violins, mostly played by rock and jazz violinists, generally work on the same principle as electric guitars. They come in all kinds of shapes, and instead of a sound-box they often have a solid or near-solid body.

Pickups
The vibrations of the strings of an electric violin are transmitted to an amplifier by two built-in pickups (see also pages 75 and 76).

Endless

You can experiment endlessly with electric violins, and people do. There are instruments available in the oddest shapes and sizes, with and without frets, and with five, six or even seven strings. And you can get all kinds of sounds and effects from an electric violin if it has MIDI and can be connected to a synthesizer. You can buy an electric violin from around £350/$500, but the top models can easily cost five times as much. Four of the better-known makes are Boston, Fender (the guitar makers), Skyinbow and Zeta. You can also make an ordinary violin 'electric': see pages 75 and 76.

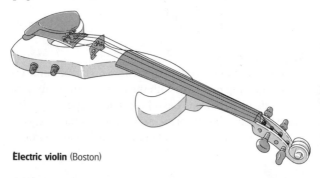

Electric violin (Boston)

Study in silence

Some types of electric violins were mainly designed for silent study. They come with a small in-built amplifier that allows you to hear your playing through a pair of headphones. You can usually add a little reverb to give the sound a bit more life. This type of violin can often be connected to a CD-player or a personal stereo so that you can play along to other music. The Yamaha Silent Violin is the best-known example.

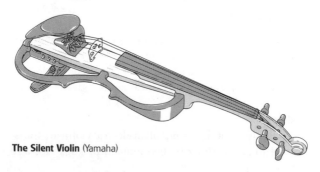

The Silent Violin (Yamaha)

13. HOW THEY'RE MADE

Violins are still made in much the same fashion as they have been for hundreds of years, with chisels and files, saws, planes and glue. A master violin maker will take several days to make the belly alone.

In a violin factory machines are used for parts of the process, such as roughly shaping all the wooden components. The 'real' violin maker, who builds an instrument him- or herself from start to finish, still does everything by hand.

Cake

Quarter-sawn wood

The belly and back are usually made of quarter-sawn wood. This means wood is sawn from a log in the shape of slices of cake. Each slice is then sawn almost in half to help the wood to dry, which makes it less likely to warp or split. This slice is later sawn through completely to make two separate halves. The two halves are then glued together by the longest edge, the beginnings of a plate (belly or back). Not all plates are made of two such halves, but most are.

Carved

The plate is carved into shape with chisels and planes. No press is used. Using moulds and thickness gauges (*graduation calipers*), and simply by feel, the violin maker keeps checking to see if any more wood needs to be removed.

105

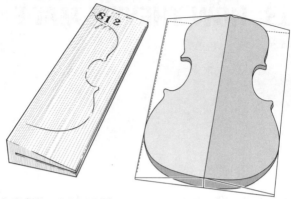

Cut in half, and glued together

The ribs

The ribs of the instrument are first shaped by heat and moisture and then glued to blocks to strengthen them at the joins. The rib structure is assembled around a mould, which is of course later removed.

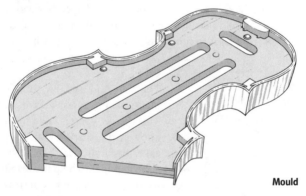

Mould

The holes, the purfling and the bass-bar

The *f*-holes and the channel for the purfling are also cut by hand. The bass-bar takes a long time to make because it has to fit the inside arch of the belly exactly.

Jigsaw puzzle

The neck and scroll are carved from a single block of wood. The shoulder of the neck slots into a block at the top of the body (the top-block) like a piece in a jigsaw puzzle. The fingerboard is made lighter by hollowing out the underside.

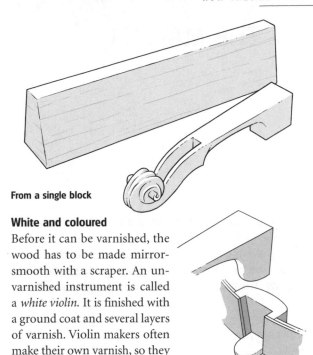

From a single block

White and coloured

Before it can be varnished, the wood has to be made mirror-smooth with a scraper. An un-varnished instrument is called a *white violin*. It is finished with a ground coat and several layers of varnish. Violin makers often make their own varnish, so they can give it exactly the colour they are looking for.

Jigsaw puzzle...

The secret

There are lots of far-fetched stories told about the secret of those expensive old Italian violins. For instance, it is said that the wood used to make them was transported by dragging it behind a sailing ship, and that it is the sea-salt that gives the violins their special sound. Others say that the wood came from centuries-old church towers which had burned down; it was 'broken in' by vibrations from the church bells and then ripened by the fire… In the end, it is perhaps the varnish which is the greatest 'secret' of those old violins, and that's probably just because the makers used ingredients that are no longer available.

Bows

To end this chapter, the bow. The bow stick is cut by hand and shaped over a flame. The horsehair is held in place in the frog and head by small wooden wedges.

14. THE MAKERS

You'll find more different names on violins than on most other instruments. Names of hundreds of violin makers young, old and dead, names of makers who never even lived, brand names and names of countries, towns and regions. The cheapest violins often have no name at all.

There are plenty of hefty books where you'll find stories of violin makers; where and when they lived and worked, as well as what their instruments could be worth. Even then, there's a good chance that the maker of your old violin won't be mentioned, simply because there are so many of them.

No name

Cheap factory violins with no name at all are usually built by firms not particularly proud of the instruments they build. However, when it comes to German-made violins it's a completely different story: there is hardly a factory-made violin from that country which doesn't say 'made in Germany'. The country has a good reputation for making violins at all price ranges.

Brand names

Sometimes the same brand name is given to violins made by a whole group of different smaller workshops or factories. In fact, one brand name may be used for violins with components from three different countries, which are assembled in a fourth country and varnished in a fifth. And then there are 'makers' who actually do little more than finishing and varnishing white factory-made violins (see page 107).

The countries

Apart from Germany, where violins have been built in numbers for hundreds of years, most affordable instruments come from China, Korea and other Asian countries, and from the Czech Republic, Hungary, Romania and Bulgaria.

Asia

Violins from China and other Asian countries have long had a poor reputation, but their quality is improving – some brands faster than others. Most of these instruments sell for around £700/$1000. German wood may be used for the better models. Asian violins are often given German names, because they 'sound better'. One of the better-known Japanese makes is **Suzuki**.

Germany

Germany produces violins in every price range, from those made by master makers to cheaper factory-made instruments. The towns of **Bubenreuth**, **Mittenwald**, and **Klingenthal** and **Markneukirchen** in Saxony are famous for their violin-making traditions and for the instruments still made there. A good, hundred-year-old factory violin from there costs between £650–1000/$1000–1500. The cheapest German violins start at around £150/$250, including bow and case.

Eastern Europe

Many of the founders of the bigger German firms originally came from Luby, also known as the Czech Mittenwald. Other Eastern European countries, such as Hungary and Romania, also have long violin-making traditions and produce instruments of all qualities.

France

France no longer produces large numbers of violins, but some two centuries ago the French town of **Mirecourt** was home to the world's first real violin factory, employing some six hundred people. Mirecourt was the most important French centre for violin-making. The prices of old French factory instruments are usually a little higher than those of comparable German violins. Because the French violins sound a little louder, some say, although others claim that they sound a little softer…

Other countries

In most countries you'll be able to find luthiers who make instruments entirely by hand, usually to order. Most of them also sell used instruments, bows and accessories, and they repair and rebuild instruments too.

Violin makes

There are endless makes of violin, as you will see if you glance through any catalogue, but some of the best known are Lidl, Knilling, Cremona, F. Cervini, H. Siegler, Anton Breton and Mathias Thoma from the USA, and Gewa, Höfner, Paesold and Ernst Roth from Germany. You may find that some of them will be more easily available than others, depending on where you live.

OLD MASTERS

Many books have been written about the classic violin makers. Here you can meet some of the most famous.

Italy

The most famous Italian violins were built from the sixteenth century onwards in the town of Cremona. **Andrea Amati** (1525–1611) was one of the first violin makers, and his grandson **Nicolo Amati** taught the craft to **Francesco Ruggieri** (1620–c.1695), the most famous member of another important Cremonese violin-making family. Another of Nicolo's pupils was **Antonio Stradivari** (Stradivarius), who lived from 1644 to 1737. Apart from violins and cellos, Stradivarius also made harps and guitars. Of his bowed instruments, around six hundred have survived. In turn, he taught the craft to **Joseph Guarnerius del Gesu** (1698–1744), who would eventually become the best-known member of the Guarnerius violin-making family. Another famous pupil of Stradivarius was **Carlo Bergonzi**.

Outside Cremona

Apart from the Cremonese school or style, to which all of these violin makers belonged, there were also Venetian, Milanese and other schools. Each one naturally had its own characteristics, such as the shape of the *f*-holes and the precise modelling of the body.

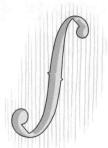

The shape of the ƒ-holes

Germany

Jacob Stainer, who died in 1683, is often seen as the founder of German violin-making. Until well into the eighteenth century a violin made by Stainer was more expensive than a Stradivarius, which was often regarded as 'too loud'. Today, a good Stainer is worth over a hundred thousand pounds or dollars. **Mathias Klotz I** (1656–1743), an important figure in the Mittenwald school, studied under Stainer and Nicolo Amati. Instruments made by the slightly younger **Sebastian Klotz** are still highly prized. One of the major violin-making dynasties in the German town of Klingenthal was the **Hopf** family, including **Caspar** (1650–1711) and his grandson **David**.

The Netherlands

Violins were also built in the Netherlands during this time, and hundreds of violin makers are known. Two of the most famous were **Hendrik Jacobs** (1630–1704) and **Johannes Cuypers** (1724–1808). Their instruments fetch anything up to £37,500/$50,000.

France

Two important French violin makers are **Nicolas Lupot** (1758–1824) and, from Mirecourt, **Jean Baptiste Vuillaume** (1798–1875). All together there were as many as thirty Vuillaumes who built violins.

England

The best-known English violin maker is **Hill**. The bows made by Hill are famous, and you very often come across the description 'Hill model' on tailpieces, tuning pegs and other components.

GLOSSARY AND INDEX

This glossary contains short definitions of all the violin-related words used in this book. There are also some words you won't find in these pages, but which you might well come across in magazines and catalogues. The page numbers tell you where in this book you can find more information on the subject.

Action *(33–34, 92)* The distance from the strings to the fingerboard, measured at the end nearest the bridge.

Adjuster *(10–11, 56, 86)* The adjuster is used to tension and relax the ribbon of the bow. Also called *end screw* or *screw button.*

Alpaca See: *Nickel silver.*

Antiquing *(27)* Technique to make violins look older than they are.

Bass-bar *(9)* Wooden bar on the inside of the belly.

Belly *(5–6, 29, 30)* One of the most important components of a violin: the upper *plate* of the body.

The opposite plate is called the back.

Body *(5–6, 29–31)* The body amplifies the sound of your violin.

Bow Violins and violas are played with a bow. This bow is very important to the sound of the instrument and the way it plays. See also: *Ribbon*, *Frog* and *Stick.*

Bow grip See: *Lapping.*

Bow stick See: *Stick.*

Bridge *(6–7, 34–35, 92–93)* The strings run over the bridge, which stands on the belly on two feet. The bridge passes the vibrations of the strings on to the soundbox.

Case See: *Violin case.*

Catgut *(46)* The oldest material used for violin strings. The name comes from *cattle gut*, although actually sheep gut is used. See also: *Strings.*

Cello *(2, 100, 101)* String instrument sounding an octave lower than a viola.

Channel *(6, 8, 30)* The 'valley' near the edge of both the belly and the back before the upward arching begins.

Cheeks *(6, 44)* The sides of the pegbox.

Children's violins *(13, 52)* Violins in small sizes.

Chin rest *(6, 8, 64–67)* The chin rest sits beside or above the tailpiece.

Curl See: *Figured wood.*

Damper See: *Mute.*

Double bass *(2, 99, 100, 101)* The lowest-sounding member of the string family.

D-ring See: *Frog.*

Ebony See: *Wood.*

Electric violin *(76, 103–104)* An electric violin can be plugged straight into an amplifier, just like an electric guitar. You can also use it to practice without anyone hearing you.

End-button *(7–8)* Small button at the bottom of the violin.

End screw See: *Adjuster.*

Eye, eyelet, Parisian eye *(37)* Inlaid decoration. A Parisian eye is a circle of mother-of-pearl with a small metal ring around it. You'll see them on tuning pegs and tailpieces, frogs and bow adjusters.

Ferrule See: *Frog.*

ƒ-hole *(5, 6, 34)* The sound-holes of a violin are shaped like an ƒ.

Figured wood *(27)* Many violins have a back and ribs which look as though they are being 'licked by flames'. Figured, or *flamed* wood is usually more expensive. The *figure*, the flame shape or 'tiger stripe', is also known as the *curl*.

Fine tuners *(6–7, 36–39, 51, 84, 91)* Small tuning mechanisms in the tailpiece. Also known as *tuning* *adjusters, string tuners* and *string adjusters.*

Fingerboard *(5–6, 31–33, 93–94)* When you play, you press down or *stop* the strings against the finger-board with your fingers to produce the various pitches on each string.

Flamed wood See: *Figured wood.*

Fractional sizes *(13, 52)* Violins and violas in small sizes, mostly played by children.

Frog *(10, 54–56, 86)* The ribbon of your bow is held in place inside the frog, which you can move for-wards or backwards by turning the adjuster. At the bottom of the frog is the *slide.* Most frogs are *fully-lined* with a metal *back-plate.* At the front, where the ribbon enters the frog, it passes through the *ferrule* or *D-ring.*

Full-size violin *(13)* The 'ordinary' and largest size of violin. See also: *Children's violins.*

German silver See: *Nickel silver.*

Hand-crafted violins *(22)* Built by a master violin maker from start to finish. This type of instrument will usually cost at least £5000/$7000.

Headstock The part of the violin at the top of the neck which includes the pegbox and scroll.

Heel *(8)* Semicircular projection of the back.

Humidity *(95–96)* The amount of moisture in the air. Violins don't like the air to be too moist, or too dry.

Hygrometer *(74, 95)* A device that measures the humidity.

Insurance *(96)* A good idea.

Lapping *(10–11, 57)* Piece of (synthetic) leather around the stick of the bow. Also called *thumb grip* or *bow grip.*

Listening tips *(42–43)* Tips on what to listen out for when you hear a violin being played.

Luthier *(22, 110)* Another name for a violin maker.

Mensur ratio See: *Scale.*

Metronome *(19)* Device which produces ticks or beeps in the tempo you want.

Mounting *(54–55)* The metal parts of a bow.

Mute *(17, 69–71)* A mute makes your sound a little sweeter and softer. *Practice mutes* muffle the sound a lot.

Neck *(6–7, 31–33)* The neck connects the body with the *headstock* of the violin. The fingerboard is attached to the neck.

Neck angle *(8, 33)* The angle between the neck and the top edge of the body.

Nickel silver *(55)* Mixture of copper, zinc and nickel. Also known as *alpaca* or *German silver*.

Nut *(6–7, 32–34)* The wooden strip over which the strings run at the top end of the neck. Also called the *top nut*.

Peg See: *Tuning peg*.

Peg compound, peg paste or peg dope *(84)* Lubricant for tuning pegs.

Pegbox *(5–6)* The tuning pegs fit into the pegbox. See: *Tuning peg*.

Pickup *(75–76, 103)* Small, thin plates of a vibration-sensitive material which convert the vibrations of the strings into electrical signals, so that you can plug your violin into an amplifier. You can fit them yourself, or buy an instrument which has pickups built in.

Plain string *(48)* Unwound string. The high E-string is usually a plain string. See: *Winding 2*.

Plates *(2–8, 44, 105)* A violin has two plates: the belly and the back.

Practice mute See: *Mute*.

Purfling *(6, 8, 28)* Narrow inlaid decoration and protection for the belly and back.

Quarter-sawn *(105)* If you saw a tree trunk or sections of it into quarters or smaller fractions (the way you would cut a cake into slices), you get stronger wood than if you *slab-cut* the tree. Because quarter-sawn wood is stronger, it is good for making thin yet strong bellies and backs.

Ribbon *(10–11, 57, 85–86)* The hairs of your bow.

Ribs *(31)* The *sides* of the body.

Rosin *(11, 61–63, 85–86)* Without rosin, your bow will do nothing at all.

Saddle *(67)* A strip, usually of ebony, which prevents the belly from being damaged by the tailgut which holds the tailpiece in place. Also known as *bottom nut.*

Scale *(14)* The scale or *scaling* of a string instrument usually indicates the *speaking length* of the strings, the part of the strings between the nut and the bridge. The word may also be used to indicate the distance from the nut to the body, the distance from the body to the bridge, or the ratio between the two. In violins that ratio, also known as the *mensur ratio*, is usually 2:3 (13:19.5 cm).

Screw button See: *Adjuster.*

Scroll *(5–7, 28)* The scroll or *volute* is a decoration at the top of the neck. Also known as the maker's signature.

Shoulder rest *(8, 67–69)* Ranging from simple pads or cushions to complicated adjustable supports.

Silent violin *(18)* A violin without a soundbox for silent practice.

Slab-cut See: *Quarter-sawn.*

Sleeves *(52, 90–91)* Protect the bridge from the strings, and the other way around.

Slide See: *Frog.*

Soundpost *(9, 36, 93)* Thin, round piece of wood wedged between belly and back near the bridge, on the side of the thinnest string.

Stick *(10, 54, 55, 56)* The wooden part of your bow.

Stradivarius *(29, 100, 110)* Antonio Stradivari was the world's most famous violin-maker. He also built the standard model for the cello.

String adjusters See: *Fine tuners.*

String length *(14)* The length of the strings between nut and bridge. See also: *Scale.*

String tuners See: *Fine tuners.*

Strings *(11, 100)*, **replacing strings** *(86–92)* There are violin strings of gut, synthetic material and metal, and with windings made of all kinds of metals.

Table See: *Belly.*

Tailgut *(6–8, 93)* The loop which attaches the tailpiece to the end-button.

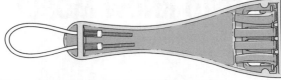

Tailpiece with adjustable tailgut and built-in fine tuners

Tailpiece *(6–8, 37, 39–40)* The strings are attached to the tailpiece, and the tailpiece is attached to the end-button.

Thumb grip See: *Lapping.*

Top See: *Belly.*

Top nut See: *Nut.*

Tuning *(36, 77–81)* Violins are tuned using the tuning pegs or the fine tuners.

Tuning adjusters See: *Fine tuners.*

Tuning peg *(5–6, 36–37, 84–85, 91)* Violins are tuned using four tuning pegs around which the strings are wrapped, sometimes in combination with one or more fine tuners. Often simply called a peg. See also: *Fine tuners.*

Varnish *(26–27)* The varnish used is important for the sound and the appearance of your violin, and for the way you need to clean it.

Viola *(9, 11, 29)* A viola is a little larger than a violin, and it sounds lower.

Violin case *(72–73)* The most important accessory for violinists.

Volute See: *Scroll.*

Winding 1. The wire or thread wound onto the bow next to the lapping *(11, 57)*. **2.** The thin wires wound around most strings *(47, 48, 49–50)*. See also: *Plain string.*

Wolf-note, Wolf-note eliminator *(69, 72)* A wolf-note is a stuttering note which is quite rare in violins but less so in cellos. Wolf-notes can be cured using a wolf-note eliminator, which 'kills' the stuttering effect.

Wood *(30, 36)* All kinds of wood are used in violin-making. For example, spruce for the belly, maple for the back, the ribs and bridge, and ebony, rosewood and boxwood for tuning pegs, tailpieces and chin rests. The fingerboard is usually made of ebony.

WANT TO KNOW MORE?

Because violins have been around for so long and because they are so expensive, because there are so many secrets and stories about them, and simply because there's so much to say about them, there's much, much more for you to read about. With the basic knowledge from this book, you'll find most books and articles about violins a lot easier to read. And of course, there's lots more information to be found on the Internet too.

MAGAZINES

The magazines listed here are only available on subscription, not in the shops.

- *STRINGS*, PO Box 151049, San Rafael, CA 94915, USA, phone: 001 415 485 6946, fax: 001 415 485 0831, email: subs.st@stringletter.com, Web site: www.stringsmagazine.com. American; comparable to The Strad.

- The Strad, 7, St John's Rd, Harrow, Middlesex HA1 2EE, United Kingdom, phone: 0044 20 863 2020, fax: 0044 20 863 2444, email: subs@thestrad.demon.co.uk, Web site: www. orphpl.com/strad.htm. Packed with information, articles and advertisements about violins, violin makers, strings, playing and much more.

BOOKS

There are dozens of books you can buy, on everything to do with violins. The titles of a few reasonably straightforward and interesting books are listed below, as is the title of a violin encyclopaedia on CD-ROM.

- *Cambridge Companion to the Violin*, Robin Stowell (Cambridge University Press, 1992/1998; UK). History, repertoire, technique and acoustics of the instrument.

- *The Violin Explained; Components, Mechanism and Sound,* James Beament (Clarendon Press, UK, 1977). For those who want to know the real details. An expensive book, but written in an accessible style, without mathematical formulas.
- *The Violin* – Multimedia Encyclopaedia (Accord Parfait, Editions Montparnasse, France, 1997). CD-ROM with music and information.
- *Violin and Viola,* Yehudi Menuhin and William Primrose (Kahn & Arwill, 1991). Mainly about playing, but also about the instrument, studying and music written for the instrument.

INTERNET

The Internet offers a huge amount of reading matter. If you go looking for everything there is on the violin or viola, you'll easily get a few hundred thousand pages to choose from! It's easier to start with one of the following Web sites, which also have Frequently Asked Questions sections and links to countless other sites. These kinds of addresses change very often, but with a bit of luck at least one of the four will give you a good start.

- Maestronet: www.maestronet.com
- Sheila's Corner: www.bright.net/~hhelser/violinsources.html
- David T. van Zandt: www.seatac.net/dtvz/
- The World of Violins: www.violink.com/

Names

Of course, you can also check out whether there is anything on the maker of your violin by searching on that name. If you are interested in the great old masters, take a look at The Smithsonian Institute's site at www.si.edu/resource/faq/nmah/music.htm#Violins

ESSENTIAL DATA

In the event of your equipment being stolen or lost, or if you decide to sell it, it's useful to have all the relevant data close to hand. Here are three pages for those notes. For the insurance company, for the police or just for yourself. And if you put new strings on your violin, you can note that information here too.

INSURANCE

Company:

Phone:

Fax:

Agent:

Phone: Fax:

Policy number:

Insured amount:

INSTRUMENTS AND ACCESSORIES

You'll find some of the details of your violin on the label, if there is one. If there is, it'll usually be under the *f*-hole on the side of the thick strings. There are also violins whose labels you can only read if the body is opened. Sometimes the name of the maker is branded on the body, for example on the back, close to the heel.

Make and model:

Manufacturer/violin maker:

Serial number:

Colour:

Make of bridge:

Tailpiece   make:

                 type:

                 colour/material:

Chin rest	make:
	type:
	colour/material:

Shoulder rest	make:
	type:
	colour/material:

Description of tuning pegs:

Any repairs, damage or other distinguishing features:

Date of purchase: price:

Place of purchase:

Phone: Fax:

STRINGS

Note down here the strings you fit to your instrument. If you like them you'll be able to buy the same ones later, or try different ones if you don't.

string	violin/viola	make	type	thickness/tension	date
1st	E/A				
2nd	A/D				
3rd	D/G				
4th	G/C				

string	violin/viola	make	type	thickness/tension	date
1st	E/A				
2nd	A/D				
3rd	D/G				
4th	G/C				

string	violin/viola	make	type	thickness/tension	date
1st	E/A				
2nd	A/D				
3rd	D/G				
4th	G/C				

ADDITIONAL NOTES

....

....

....

....

....

....

....

....

....

....

....

....

....

....

ROUGH GUIDE
Music Books
Music Reference Guides

Essential CD Guides

Mini Guides

ROUGH GUIDE
Instrument Guides

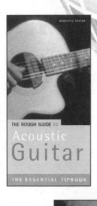

THE ROUGH GUIDE TO
Acoustic Guitar
THE ESSENTIAL TIPBOOK

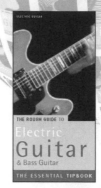

THE ROUGH GUIDE TO
Electric Guitar
& Bass Guitar
THE ESSENTIAL TIPBOOK

THE ROUGH GUIDE TO
Piano
THE ESSENTIAL TIPBOOK

THE ROUGH GUIDE TO
Keyboards
& Digital Piano
THE ESSENTIAL TIPBOOK

THE ROUGH GUIDE TO
Saxophone
THE ESSENTIAL TIPBOOK

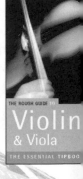

THE ROUGH GUIDE TO
Violin
& Viola
THE ESSENTIAL TIPBOOK

ESSENTIAL TIPBOOK
SERIES

Coming in 2001

Clarinet   Flute